AMAZING AND EXTRAORDINARY FACTS

CATHEDRALS
AND ABBEYS

CATHEDRALS
AND ABBEYS

Stephen Halliday

RP
RYDON
PUBLISHING

A Rydon Publishing Book
35 The Quadrant
Hassocks
West Sussex
BN6 8BP
www.rydonpublishing.co.uk
www.rydonpublishing.com

First published by Rydon Publishing in 2015

A CIP catalogue record for this book is available from the British Library.

ISBN: 978-1-910821-04-6

Printed in Great Britain by Polestar Wheatons

CONTENTS

INTRODUCTION

Great Britain and Ireland are particularly well endowed with cathedrals and abbeys. Many of them are buildings that have their origins in Roman Britain, while others are fine examples of modern architecture – yet each has its own rich and sometimes bloody history. Many of our older cathedrals and abbeys were built by the Normans, for William the Conqueror was more than generous in awarding bishoprics, which were often lucrative, to his followers.

But what is a cathedral? In answer it is the principal church of a diocese, one of the primary units of administration in the Christian church. It is therefore where the seat of the diocesan bishop is found, the word 'cathedral' itself being derived from a Greek word that means 'seat'. In a few cases a cathedral is the principal place of worship within an archdiocese headed by an archbishop, as is the case with Canterbury and York for the Church of England, also known as the Anglican Church. Although the bishop is in charge of the diocese, the cathedral itself is headed by a dean – sometimes called a provost.

It is commonly believed that the presence of an Anglican cathedral in a town automatically brings it city status. It is certainly true that some small communities like St Davids in Wales – with a population of fewer than 2,000 people, thus smaller than some villages – owes its city status to the presence of its cathedral. But as we shall see, city status does not necessarily follow. And some places, like Cambridge, became cities without a cathedral because the monarch issued a charter to make them so.

Meanwhile an abbey is a church, which in origin at least was built in conjunction with a monastery, friary or convent. All these followed in some form the Rule of St Benedict, which required them to follow a life of prayer governed by the virtues of poverty, chastity and obedience. Some communities were little more than comfortable homes for the nobility, offering lives of luxury. For example Ely Cathedral was preceded by an abbey, whose first three abbesses, including the founder Etheldreda, were widowed queens who would have expected to live in some comfort. Other religious communities were far more austere, such as the Cistercians, of whom we will hear more.

So how many cathedrals are there? The answer depends on whom you ask, and on which Christian groups you include. The obvious candidates are the Anglican Church and the Roman Catholic Church. But what about the Ukrainian Autocephalous Church and its Belorussian equivalent? Or the Antiochian Orthodox Church? Not to mention the Ancient Catholic Church, and the quite distinct Ancient and *Old* Catholic Church. Not to forget the Anglican Catholic Church and the Traditional Church of England – the latter has its cathedral at Windlesham in Surrey and shows a marked reluctance to admit women to the priesthood.

In this volume we will focus on the Anglican cathedrals of England with brief excursions to Wales, Scotland and Ireland, as well as nods in the direction of the Roman Catholic cathedrals, the selection being based on the historic associations and architectural qualities of the buildings.

Abbeys present a different problem. It is estimated that there were almost 1,000 of these in England and Wales during the Middle Ages. Then Thomas Cromwell closed the great majority of them during the dissolution of the monasteries that followed the break with Rome in the reign of Henry VIII. Thanks to Cromwell, many of the most remarkable monasteries are now ruins, the monks are dispersed, and their magnificent abbeys have fallen into disuse.

Some were plundered by local inhabitants to build their own palaces. Meanwhile others survived because their local communities adopted them as parish churches. The outstanding example is St Albans (always spelt without an apostrophe), which was founded as an abbey for the monastery to commemorate England's first Christian martyr, and which then became the parish church of the adjacent town when the abbey was dissolved in 1539.

The sources I have consulted for this volume are too numerous to mention. They include many websites, and more books from Cambridge University Library than there is space to list. Any errors are likely to be mine.

Stephen Halliday, May 2015

ST ALBANS CATHEDRAL

Off with his head!
The story of the first
English martyr

The story of the current St Albans Cathedral starts with Alban (third century), who was a citizen of the Roman city Verulamium, which we now know as St Albans. Alban gave shelter to a Christian priest called Amphibalus who subsequently converted Alban to Christianity. This event probably occurred in 209, during the persecution of Christians under the rule of the Emperor Septimus Severus (193–211) of African descent, although the date is uncertain.

Alban was beheaded for his Christian faith on a hill outside Verulamium and according to legend, his head rolled down the hill, causing a well to appear where his head came to rest. The hill was subsequently named Holywell Hill, and to this day a well still exists at its foot. The historian known as the Venerable Bede (672–735), writing four centuries after the event, also claimed that the eyes of Alban's executioner fell out as he wielded the axe.

In the centuries that followed a series of Christian places of worship, including a shrine, were erected close to the site of Alban's execution, the early ones being created quite shortly after the execution itself. Bede refers to a church on the site that became known as St Albans while others mention a shrine. Later Matthew Paris, a monk at St Albans, claimed Saxon invaders destroyed the buildings that surrounded the shrine in 586.

St Alban

A NAME-DROPPING MONK

Matthew Paris (1200–59) entered St Albans Abbey as a monk in 1217 and devoted his life, as many monks did, to writing – in his case works of history. These included the **Chronica Majora** *– a history of the world no less, from the creation to 1253 – the* **Life of Saint Alban** *and works on several other saints. He was very well connected, often using material supplied to him by royalty and nobility; he was also a great gossip and name-dropper.*

His works are much used by historians of the period, yet treated with some scepticism since much of his material is of very doubtful authenticity. However there is no doubt he was a better historian than artist – he drew a picture of an elephant that was the first ever seen in England, which Louis IX of France gave Henry III in 1253, but in this picture he had given the elephant horses' hooves!

Not suitable for the role
The English Pope who didn't bear a grudge

Nicholas Breakspear (c. 1100–59) was born in Abbots Langley, close to St Albans in Hertfordshire, to a father who later became a monk of the abbey himself. When Nicholas applied to follow his father into the monastery he was told by the abbot to 'wait to go on with his schooling so that he might be considered more suitable'. Thus Nicholas travelled to France, Scandinavia and Italy to follow his calling, eventually being elected as the Pope in 1154 – the only Englishman ever to hold that office.

Pope Adrian IV, as Nicholas became, obviously didn't bear a grudge since one of his first acts as the Pope was to declare the abbot of St Albans as the 'premier abbot of England'. This greatly enhanced the abbey's status as an important shrine and guaranteed a steady flow of pilgrims, not to mention money. It is fascinating to learn that the family who founded Breakspear's brewery in Henley-on-Thames are related to the Pope!

Nicholas Breakspear, who became Pope Adrian IV

BUT HE HAS A LOT TO ANSWER FOR!

Soon after he became the Pope, Adrian allegedly invited Henry II of England to invade Ireland in order to bring its churches under the authority of Rome. Thus began an English involvement in Irish affairs, with all the consequences that followed. It seems that Nicholas Breakspear has much to answer for!

A conspicuous feature
The Christian shrine built from Roman bricks

King Offa of Mercia (d. 796), better known for his dyke, built an early abbey at St Albans in 793 that was later sacked by the Danes. Thus it was Paul of Caen, the first Norman abbot who held the position between 1077 and 1093, who was largely responsible for construction of the building we know now. Much of the material used in the Norman abbey was plundered from the ruins of Roman Verulamium, making use of its Roman bricks.

The Romans brought the art of brickmaking to Britain, but took it home with them when they abandoned the province in 410. It was not rediscovered until about 1400, so there are in fact very few medieval buildings in England constructed of brick and those that do exist are mostly built from recycled Roman ones. These Roman bricks are a conspicuous feature of St Albans Cathedral, recognizable as they are longer and thinner than later versions. So it is ironic that the

Romans, who executed St Alban, actually provided the bricks to build his cathedral!

FACELESS THOMAS

In 1539 the abbey was surrendered to Henry VIII, who was busy dissolving and plundering England's monasteries following the break with Rome. The paintings of saints in the nave were whitewashed, and special care was taken to obliterate the face of Archbishop St Thomas à Becket – a bête noire for Henry VIII because Thomas had challenged the authority of Henry's ancestor Henry II just as Henry VIII was challenging the Pope. The paintings have been restored but poor Thomas still has no face.

Broken up
An abbey church for sale

Following the surrender of the monastery to Henry VIII, the Norman estate of St Albans was broken up. One building became a school, the gatehouse became a jail and now belongs to St Albans School, and the church was sold to the people of St Albans as a parish church – they paid £400 for the purchase. The shrine of St Alban was destroyed although the watching chamber survived – this was a room from which a monk watched the pilgrims as they visited the shrine, presumably to ensure that they didn't remove any pieces as souvenirs.

The abbey turned out to be far too large for the parishioners to support – the population of the town did not reach 10,000 until the reign of Victoria. So it was in poor condition by the 1870s when the new diocese of St Albans was carved out from the old diocese of Lincoln and the abbey became a cathedral. The diocese of Lincoln, founded in 678, once extended from the Humber estuary to the River Thames, including counties as remote as Buckinghamshire and Oxfordshire. The process of whittling it down to a manageable size began in the reign of Henry VIII when the dioceses of Oxford and Peterborough were created – in 1877 Hertfordshire finally gained its own diocese, based at St Albans.

Force of nature
Baron Grimthorpe to the rescue

When St Albans became a cathedral in 1877 it was sadly in no condition to assume its newly elevated status. A survey carried out after part of the building collapsed revealed that much of it was a ruin. Several thousand pounds were raised to restore the building and work proceeded slowly under the supervision of the celebrated Victorian architect George Gilbert Scott until his death in 1878.

Following the death of George Gilbert Scott a force of nature was to descend upon St Albans in the form of Edmund Beckett Denison, 1st Baron Grimthorpe (1816–1905). As an extremely wealthy barrister, amateur horologist – he designed the Parliamentary clock commonly referred to as Big Ben – and amateur architect of strong opinions, he offered to fund the reconstruction of the new cathedral, providing that his own designs were adopted.

Denison was a self-righteous bully, and in the *Dictionary of National Biography* he is described as being notable for his 'powers of sarcasm and assertive manner'. Some idea of his appalling character may be gained from a series of offensive letters he wrote to *The Times* regarding Sir Charles Barry, architect of the Houses of Parliament, who was trying to work harmoniously with Denison to accommodate the latter's clock design. Following a letter from Denison referring to 'the stupidity of Sir C. Barry', *The Times* declined to publish any more correspondence. In addition, although the Horological Institute elected Denison as their president in recognition of his work, they wisely stipulated that he be forbidden to attend their dinners to avoid the arguments that would surely follow!

Denison demolished the west end of the cathedral and replaced it with his own design. This has been described as 'Victorian Disney Gothic', with embellishments of the kind much appreciated by Hollywood film producers who have been known to make use of the cathedral for filming. It is easy to criticize Denison, as many have done, but without him and the £130,000 he spent on

Grimthorpe's West End at St Albans

restoration the cathedral might not have survived at all.

AN ARCHITECTURAL DYNASTY

There will be many references throughout this book to the Scott family who were major contributors both to restoring and designing ecclesiastical buildings. Sir George Gilbert Scott (1811–78) was one of the most famous architects of the Victorian period, being closely associated with the revival of Gothic forms of architecture. St Pancras Station Hotel and the Albert Memorial are notable examples of his work, but he also worked on well over a hundred churches, abbeys and cathedrals, either building or restoring them.

His son, also George Gilbert Scott (1839–97), followed his father into the profession, and although less well known than his illustrious father, he nevertheless designed a number of fine buildings for three Cambridge colleges – namely Pembroke, Christ's and Peterhouse – before succumbing to alcoholism and dying in the St Pancras Station Hotel, which his father had designed. Then his son, Sir Giles Gilbert Scott (1880–1960), continued the family tradition, designing Cambridge University Library, Liverpool's Anglican cathedral, Battersea Power Station and the famous red telephone box. Giles's brother, Adrian Scott, submitted a design for the Catholic cathedral in Liverpool, however it was not adopted (see 'Paddy's Wigwam').

A new shrine
With a shoulder blade attached

Later architects have been more sympathetic to the Norman building of St Albans Cathedral (see 'Force of nature') – indeed Elizabeth II opened a new visitor centre in 1982 built from replica Roman bricks. St Alban's shrine was reconstructed in 1993 from fragments that had been abandoned by the Tudor iconoclasts and were rediscovered during the Victorian restoration. Furthermore in 2002 a shoulder blade, believed to be a relic of St Alban, was presented to the cathedral by a church in Cologne, Germany that had owned it for about 1,000 years. The feast day of St Alban is still celebrated each year on 22 June.

WHY NOT A PATRON SAINT?
The patron saint of England is St George who, if he existed at all, was probably born in Turkey and is no more likely to have visited these lands than he is to have killed a dragon. He is also, more appropriately, the patron saint of Georgia. Would it not be sensible for us to let the Georgians have him and to adopt St Alban in his place? To this day, Anglican churches are only permitted by law to fly the flag of St George. Few people know this law, while even fewer observe it.

BATH ABBEY

Throne in a spa
Ten centuries of coronations

Bath has been a spa since the Romans discovered its hot springs – it is less often associated with coronations. Yet King Edgar the Peaceful, the great-grandson of Alfred the Great and father of Ethelred the Unready, was crowned King of the English in Bath Abbey in 973, the abbey itself having been founded about 400 years earlier by Osric (otherwise little known to history), King of the Hwicce (equally unknown to history, with their capital at Worcester).

On 2 June 1953, 980 years later, Harold Bradfield, Bishop of Bath and Wells, was seen accompanying Elizabeth II at her coronation in

Westminster Abbey. The reason for this is that the Bishop of Bath and Wells, along with the Bishop of Durham, has the privilege of accompanying the monarch within Westminster Abbey for the coronation ceremony. This privilege is recorded in the Red Book of coronation practices, which is held by the Dean of Westminster and has been compiled over centuries by the deans and their predecessors, the abbots of Westminster.

Follow the money
Abbey, cathedral or church?

E ven by the extraordinary standards of other ecclesiastical buildings, Bath Abbey has experienced an unusually chequered history. Over the 14 centuries of its existence it has been, variously: an abbey; a convent; a monastery; the seat of a bishop; a cathedral; a ruin; a rebuilt cathedral; a parish church; and finally a parish church that is also an abbey, which shares a bishop with Wells.

William the Conqueror's son, William II, granted the City and

Abbey of Bath to a royal physician named John of Tours (died 1122). The abbey was one of the wealthiest in the kingdom, and John the royal physician soon became John, Bishop of Wells and Abbot of Bath. However the city of Bath had its own mint, so attracted by this additional source of revenue, John moved the seat of his bishopric from Wells to Bath.

He thereby became the first Bishop of Bath – Wells was not happy about this – and he raised the abbey to the rank of a cathedral. In accordance with its new status, John used his newly found wealth to rebuild the abbey on a much grander scale. When he died in 1122 he was buried in his part-built cathedral.

Decision time
Bishops on the move

T he Norman construction of Bath Abbey was completed in about 1150, following which a succession of bishops had great difficulty in deciding where to live. After a brief sojourn in Glastonbury – whose monks didn't want a bishop around the place – Jocelin, the bishop at the time, moved back to Bath. In the meantime the dispute between Bath and Wells over which was the more important rumbled on until Pope Innocent IV, in a masterly display of medieval diplomacy, appointed Roger of Salisbury as Bishop of Bath and Wells, a title that survives to this day.

Following the Pope's diplomatic triumph, later bishops found it more convenient to reside at Wells, which itself gained the status of a cathedral. The bishops occupied its magnificent Bishop's Palace, whose building was begun by Bishop Jocelin in 1201 (see 'Castle-like design'). In 2013, eight centuries after the palace was built, the Church Commissioners announced that henceforward the bishop would live in a nearby rectory. This caused much alarm both in Wells and elsewhere amidst fears that some redevelopment of this fine historic building would take place. A year later the plan was abandoned – the bishop still resides in his palace.

Bath Abbey

THE BABY-EATING BISHOP

The most notorious bishop of this diocese is without doubt the fictional Elizabethan Baby-eating Bishop of Bath and Wells. Lord Edmund Blackadder introduced him to the world when he was threatened by the bishop, who was collecting a debt on behalf of the Black Monks of St Herod. Cunning plans hatched by Baldrick and Blackadder so greatly impressed the bishop that he offered Blackadder a career in the church, an offer that was politely declined.

No swearing, please!
A beau, a rebel, the typist's friend, and a doom-monger

Bath Abbey, which became a parish church during the reign of Elizabeth I, contains many memorials, including one to Beau Nash (1674–1762), for many years the Master of Ceremonies at the spa. After a career as a soldier, a lawyer and a gambler Nash made Bath the most fashionable spa of its day by banning swearing and duelling, and by imposing his own code of dress and decorum. He even persuaded a royal physician to recommend Bath's waters for drinking and bathing, selling the tepid fluid for the outrageous price of sixpence a glass.

The abbey also contains, surprisingly, a memorial to William Bingham (1752–1804), a senator from the USA who was among those who rebelled against British rule, yet returned to England and died

Beau Nash

in Bath. And there is a memorial to Isaac Pitman, the inventor of shorthand, and the Reverend Thomas Malthus, whose gloomy and mistaken predictions of forthcoming famine were to influence the work of Charles Darwin.

Tapping the hot springs
*What did the Romans
do for Bath Abbey?*

In the context of Bath Abbey, the answer to this classic Monty Python question is that they provided a heating system. The abbey has long been infamous for its inadequate and decaying Victorian heating system, obliging winter congregations up to the present day to clad themselves in heavy coats.

Over a million litres of water at 46°C (115°F) makes its way via Roman drains into the River Avon daily, but plans are now afoot to tap the energy from the hot springs, thus providing under-floor heating for the abbey. This should annually save around £30,000 on heating oil, while providing eco-friendly warmth for the abbey and its no

longer chilled congregation, as well as for the famous Roman Baths that were built to take advantage of these hot springs. So that's what the Romans did for Bath Abbey.

BELFAST CATHEDRALS

Black Santa
An annual sit-out for charity

Belfast has two cathedrals, one for the Church of Ireland and the other that serves the city's substantial Catholic population. The Cathedral of St Anne, the cathedral that belongs to the Church of Ireland, is situated in Belfast's Cathedral Quarter and serves two dioceses, the diocese of Connor and the diocese of Down and Dromore.

The foundation stone for St Anne's was laid in 1899 and the building was completed in 1927, the west front being dedicated to the memory of the Ulstermen who died in World War I. The cathedral dedication took place on 5 July 1932, a date chosen because it was the 1,500th anniversary of St Patrick's arrival in

Ireland (see 'Protestant establishment').

Three years later the cathedral saw its first state funeral for Sir Edward Carson, who is primarily remembered for his opposition to Home Rule for Ireland, which led to the creation of Northern Ireland as a separate state. However he is also remembered for his destruction in court of the unfortunate Oscar Wilde after Wilde's disastrous decision to prosecute the Marquess of Queensberry for libel, a case that led to Wilde's disgrace and imprisonment. Carson is buried in the cathedral.

In 1976 the Reverend Samuel Crooks, Dean of St Anne's at the height of the Troubles, began what became the tradition of the Christmas 'Sit-Out' when he spent the week before Christmas sitting on the steps of the cathedral, raising money from passers-by for charities. He became known as the Black Santa because of the black coat he wore to protect him from the cold winter weather.

This tradition continues to this day, with both the current dean and other members of the cathedral clergy collecting money. Approximately £200,000 is raised each year for a variety of charities, with more than a million pounds raised in 2004 during an extended sit-out for victims of the tsunami that struck much of east Asia on Christmas Eve of that year.

In 2007, following the restoration of peace to Northern Ireland after the Troubles, the cathedral acquired a conspicuous addition in the form of a 40 metre (131 foot) stainless steel spire, named the Spire of Hope.

A PRIESTLY ARCHITECT

St Peter's is the Catholic cathedral for the diocese of Down and Connor and is located in the Divis Street area of the Falls Road, in the heart of Belfast's Catholic community. Similarly to many English cathedrals it began life as a parish church and was designed by a priest, Jeremiah Ryan McAulay, who trained as an architect before taking holy orders. In 1866 the building was consecrated as a parish church then 120 years later it became a cathedral. Much of the decoration was inspired by the Gothic Revival architect A. W. N. Pugin, who converted to Catholicism in 1834 and is chiefly remembered for his work on the internal decoration of the Houses of Parliament.

BIRMINGHAM CATHEDRAL

An unusual dedication
The small cathedral in a large city

Birmingham, England's second largest city, has one of its smallest cathedrals – only those of Derby and Chelmsford are smaller – moreover Birmingham is unique among English cathedrals in being named after St Philip. Indeed very few churches of any kind are dedicated to that rather neglected apostle. Like many cathedrals, St Philip's began life in the eighteenth century as a parish church for the small town of Birmingham. It was consecrated in 1715, its unusual dedication due to the fact that a local benefactor named Robert Philips had donated the land on which it was built.

The cathedral also enjoys the surely unique distinction of having been constructed for a quarter of its estimated price – £5,012 against the original estimate of about £20,000. Much of the shortfall was due to the fact that pious local townsfolk donated many of the materials, and of course the land. The Pre-Raphaelite artist Edward Burne-Jones (1833–98) was born in Birmingham and donated three windows to the cathedral, which are located at its eastern end, and he also designed the west window.

Birmingham enjoyed a period of almost unrivalled expansion in the nineteenth century under the dynamic leadership of Joseph Chamberlain (1836-1914). First as Mayor of Birmingham and later as President of the Board of Trade, Chamberlain was a leader in the expansion of industry, trade and empire during the reign of Victoria and later. Birmingham became a major centre for light engineering and banking so by 1889 its population and prosperity had grown to the point where it became a city, with St Philip's Church as its new cathedral.

BRISTOL CATHEDRAL

Unique among its peers
*Not a church hall but
a Hall Church*

The Church of the Holy and Undivided Trinity in Bristol became a cathedral by decree of Henry VIII in 1542, when the king and his archbishop, Thomas Cranmer (1489–1556), decided to create the new diocese of Bristol from parts of the dioceses of Gloucester, and Bath and Wells. However by the time the church became a cathedral, it was already four centuries old.

Founded in 1140 during the troubled reign of King Stephen (1135-54) as St Augustine's Abbey Church, the chapter house, which was built in the Norman style in the 1140s, has some of the earliest Gothic (pointed) arches in the world. One of its medieval stonemasons – at the time the word 'architect' had not come into use – was known as William the Geometer, a reflection of the fact that even in the Middle Ages mathematical skills were regarded as critical in the construction of complex buildings.

In addition, the building is unique among English cathedrals in being constructed as a Hall Church. That is to say it is a building in which the aisles are at the same height as the choir, providing a large open space of uniform size – a common feature of German cathedrals but very unusual in Britain.

The cathedral suffered the customary vandalism associated with the Reformation under Henry VIII and the subsequent Commonwealth in the seventeenth century, when it saw the destruction of stained glass windows and the defacement of paintings. However in the twentieth century the Lady Chapel was repainted in what were believed to be its medieval colours, guided by fragments of colour left by the iconoclasts of earlier centuries.

In 1831, during the repair work that followed a fire, a very unusual Saxon stone panel depicting Christ's Harrowing of Hell was revealed. It had been used as a coffin lid, but has now been restored to a more prominent position in the South

Transept. The cathedral contains a memorial to one of its clergy, Richard Hakluyt (1553-1616), who by his writings promoted the early settlement by English voyagers of North America and after whom the Hakluyt Society is named. There is also a monument to Robert Southey (1774–1843), friend of William Wordsworth and fellow poet of the Lake School of poetry, who was Poet Laureate for 30 years until his death.

BUCKFAST ABBEY

Monks and drunks
'And is there honey still for tea?'

Buckfast Abbey near Buckfastleigh in Devon first became an abbey with a monastery attached in 1018, during the reign of King Canute who may well have founded it. It was a Cistercian house, and like other Cistercian foundations it was deliberately built in a remote location to escape the temptations of the world. Also like other Cistercian foundations, by developing the surrounding wilderness through

hard work it became prosperous and wealthy during the five centuries of its existence. It was therefore a tempting prey for Henry VIII when it was dissolved in 1539 and was given to one of his nobles, who then used it for its stone.

However the abbey's fortunes revived when it was purchased by a group of French Benedictine monks who had fallen out with the abbot of their monastery of Sainte-Marie de la Pierre-Qui-Vire in Burgundy. The early nineteenth-century Gothic mansion that had been built on the site was incorporated into the design of the new foundation then the site was reconstituted as an abbey in 1902, nine centuries after its first foundation. The abbey church stands on the site of the Cistercian abbey.

Today the abbey has its own farm that provides food for the monks' table and is noted for two products that are more widely available. Firstly Brother Adam, of German extraction, developed a honeybee known as the Buckfast bee as the result of an extensive breeding programme. This strain of bees is still supplied to beekeepers although

'Buckie' – be warned!

brother Adam died in
1996 at 98 years old.
Better known, and
more controversial, is
Buckfast Tonic Wine,
a fortified wine with
the strength of sherry
that has been made
to a French recipe
since the 1890s. It
gained an unwanted
reputation as a cause
of violent drunken
behaviour, to the
extent that the
police in Scotland
requested that
warning notices be attached to the
bottles – not quite what one expects
from the product of a monastery!
Popularly known as 'Buckie' it is now
available for purchase on Amazon.

REMOTE BUT MAGNIFICENT

*Buckfast Abbey was not alone in
seeking and profiting from a remote
location. In some cases the remoteness
of Cistercian houses has ensured*

*that some of the buildings remained
after the Reformation, ruined but
magnificent. Fountains Abbey near
Ripon in Yorkshire, which featured
in the film* **The History Boys,** *and
Tintern Abbey in Monmouthshire are
fine examples, the latter inspiring one
of Wordsworth's most moving poems.*

*The former Prime Minister
Harold Wilson chose Rievaulx
Abbey, also in Yorkshire but this time
near Helmsley, for his title when
he became a peer – thus he became
Lord Wilson of Rievaulx. Winston
Churchill and King George VI
visited the ruins of Kirkham
Priory near Malton in North
Yorkshire in 1944 to watch the
troops who were training there for
the invasion of Normandy, using the
adjacent river Derwent to test their
landing craft.*

*The first Cistercian abbey in
England, Waverley Abbey, was
founded near Farnham in Surrey
in 1128. Dissolved in 1536, its
ruins may still be seen – the abbey
gave its name to one of Sir Walter
Scott's novels and the ruins have
frequently featured in films.*

CANTERBURY CATHEDRAL

Saints and sinners
The renegade archbishop and frustrated king

In 597 St Augustine (died c. 604) arrived in England, having been sent by Pope Gregory the Great to convert the heathen English to Christianity. In fact Christianity was already approaching from the north, led by St Columba who had arrived on the Scottish island of Iona in 563. Nevertheless Augustine duly set to work, and having landed near Margate, he baptized Aethelbert, King of Kent, then set off for Aethelbert's capital at Canterbury.

There, according to the Venerable Bede (see 'Memorials'), he built a cathedral on the foundations of a Roman temple – although it seems more likely that he simply built it beside a Roman road. A larger stone building soon followed then St Dunstan, who became Archbishop of Canterbury in 960, added an abbey and monastery. In 1011 the Vikings ransacked the cathedral, killing the

archbishop at the time, Alphege.

Then in 1067 the Saxon cathedral was destroyed by fire, so in 1070 the Norman Archbishop Lanfranc began to build a new cathedral. The chair of St Augustine in which archbishops are enthroned probably dates from this time or shortly afterwards, its first use being recorded in 1205. By that date Canterbury was becoming very wealthy, thanks to a disagreement between a notoriously bad tempered king and a turbulent archbishop.

Henry II (1133–89) was in the process of reforming the English legal system to create the common law, a uniform legal code for the whole nation – an admirable project. His problem was that a separate and much milder system of justice, known as canon law, applied to offending clergymen, known as 'criminous clerks'. Their cases were heard and sentences determined by bishops' courts, and a clergyman accused of a serious crime such as murder or rape had a much better chance of escaping severe punishment in a bishop's court than a royal one. Moreover, since anyone with a rudimentary ability to read could claim the

– 26 –

protection of the bishops' courts, this meant that many who weren't ordained clergy could escape justice.

Henry II appointed his friend Thomas à Becket (c. 1118–70) as archbishop, to the indignation of the rest of the clergy, confident that Becket would support him in his reforms. Becket was ordained priest on 2 June 1162 and became archbishop the following day – a record unlikely to be beaten. Henry must have felt confident but Becket went native, obstinately defending the separate system of canon law for priests. In frustration Henry, a notoriously foul-tempered man, cried something like 'Will no one rid me of this turbulent priest?' Eventually three of his knights murdered the archbishop in his cathedral on 29 December 1170.

In 1172 Henry II made his peace with the Pope, vowed to embark on a crusade – although he never got round to it – and allowed canon law to continue. This law was to survive in some matters into the nineteenth century, but Henry had a point!

Canterbury Cathedral

A DANGEROUS JOB

Nowadays an archbishop's job is not thought of as particularly dangerous, yet in earlier times the role of Archbishop of Canterbury certainly was. Apart from Alphege, four other archbishops of this cathedral lost their lives: Simon Sudbury was murdered by Wat Tyler's rebels in the Peasants' Revolt of 1381; Thomas Cranmer was burned in 1533 for heresy by the Catholic Queen Mary; William Laud was beheaded in 1633 for offending the Puritans; and of course, Thomas à Becket was murdered in 1170.

Good for business
*An unpopular archbishop
becomes a saint*

Thomas à Becket had not been a popular archbishop. However in little more than two years after his death at Canterbury Cathedral in 1170 (see 'Saints and sinners') he was made a saint and the place of his murder became one of the most important Christian pilgrimage sites, preceded only by Rome and Jerusalem. This brought great wealth to the cathedral and, of course, engendered Chaucer's *Canterbury Tales*, whose pilgrims set off in an epic tale for Canterbury, 'the holy, blissful martyr for to seek'; his murder also inspired T. S. Eliot's *Murder in the Cathedral*.

The money gained from the pilgrims was used to extend and rebuild the cathedral in the Gothic style from the late fourteenth century, although it retains one of the finest Norman crypts – and it is that Gothic cathedral with some later additions that we see today. During one of his forays into Scotland, Edward I, known as the Hammer of the Scots, stole the Scottish crown, presenting it as an additional embellishment to Becket's shrine.

Surprisingly, a portrait of Becket survived the Tudors and Puritans in the north aisle of the cathedral. It dates from the twelfth century, shortly after Becket's death, and is presumably a good likeness. Since Henry VIII in particular hated Becket as a churchman who had defied royal authority, we can only assume that the Tudor iconoclasts failed to recognize the portrait of the renegade archbishop. It's lucky the king didn't find out!

TERM OF ABUSE
The term 'Gothic' was coined by a sixteenth-century Italian writer of the Renaissance named Giorgio Vasari (1511–74) as a term of abuse, since he considered the style a vulgar departure from classical Greek and Roman architecture. Moreover he considered it a 'barbarous German style', which he attributed to the Gothic tribes who had invaded Europe as the Roman Empire had declined. History has decided otherwise.

The Red Dean
A socialist to the end

The Dean of Canterbury is one of the most senior figures in the Anglican Church, and as such is appointed by the monarch upon the advice of the Prime Minister then nominally elected by the canons of the cathedral chapter. The resulting appointments have not always been happy ones.

The most notorious was that of Hewlett Johnson, known as the Red Dean of Canterbury (1874–1966). After a career as a civil engineer, he became a priest in Cheshire and a strong advocate of the poor then in October 1917 he spoke in favour of the Bolshevik revolution. Despite his Bolshevik sympathies he was appointed Dean of Canterbury in 1931, and having been invited to tour the Soviet Union, wrote a highly favourable account of its economic development and the conditions of the working classes – overlooking the oppressive apparatus of the Soviet system.

As a result, Johnson was fêted in the Soviet Union – where he seems to have been confused with the Archbishop of Canterbury. He continued to argue the socialist and Soviet case, having been made a member of the Order of the Red Banner of Soviet Labour, and to infuriate the authorities of church and state until he resigned from the position of dean in 1963. He died three years later, a socialist to the end.

NOSY PARKER
When the Archbishop of Canterbury is enthroned, he takes the oath on one of the oldest books in existence in Europe, which there are strong reasons for believing once belonged to St Augustine himself. This is an illuminated copy of the four gospels written in Latin that is held in the Parker Library of Corpus Christi College, Cambridge from which it is taken to Canterbury for the ceremony.

Matthew Parker (1504–75) was a graduate of the college who was appointed Archbishop of Canterbury by Elizabeth I in 1559. She encouraged him to collect and preserve books from monastic libraries that were in danger of being lost or destroyed. This led to him visiting many establishments to enquire about these matters, which may be the origin of the expression 'Nosy Parker'. He bequeathed his invaluable collection to his college, which now houses them in its Parker Library.

CHELMSFORD CATHEDRAL

No city status
The cathedral without a city

Chelmsford Cathedral

For almost a century the people of Chelmsford in Essex had reason to feel hard done by – they weren't citizens, they were just townsfolk. Chelmsford had long been the county town of Essex and in 1914 its parish church, dedicated to St Mary, St Peter and St Cedd, became a cathedral with its own bishop when a new diocese was created. In 1938 Chelmsford City Football Club was created, the founders of the club believing reasonably but mistakenly that a county town with an Anglican cathedral was automatically a city. The name they chose was therefore wrong, but no one seemed to mind so it stuck. The coveted city status had to wait until 2012, when Elizabeth II created Essex's first city on the occasion of her Diamond Jubilee. And the townsfolk became citizens at last, after 98 years with their own cathedral.

CHESTER CATHEDRAL

A less-celebrated miracle
St Werburgh sees off a plague of geese

In 1541 Chester acquired a cathedral by order of Henry VIII.

He decreed that the former abbey church of St Werburgh, built in 1093 on the site of a basilica dating from Roman times, was to become the cathedral for the diocese of Chester.

Hugh Lupus ('Lupus' meaning 'the Wolf'), 1st Earl of Chester had built the church of St Werburgh. His descendants, also using the name Lupus, went on to become the fabulously wealthy Grosvenor family – Dukes of Westminster and owners of much of Mayfair, Belgravia and Pimlico in London.

Meanwhile St Werburgh (died 699) was an Anglo-Saxon princess credited with ridding Weedon Bec in Northamptonshire of a plague of geese – one of the less celebrated miracles in our long history! Her shrine can now be found in Chester Cathedral's Lady Chapel.

Controversial circumstances
Rebuilding rather than restoring the cathedral?

The present Chester Cathedral largely dates from the late thirteenth century to the mid-sixteenth century, although it was heavily restored in the nineteenth century by the ever-present George Gilbert Scott (see 'An architectural dynasty') in controversial circumstances. The building had been constructed of locally quarried red sandstone, which had the advantage of being fairly easy to carve, but also had the accompanying disadvantage of being easily eroded by rain and polluted air. Scott virtually re-cladded the cathedral in sandstone from Runcorn, arguing that his work

The Shrine of Werburgh at Chester Cathedral

was in keeping with the origins and character of the building.

However in 1868 Samuel Huggins, an architect from nearby Liverpool, argued that Scott was rebuilding rather than restoring the building. In 1871 Huggins wrote a treatise entitled *On So-Called Restoration of our Cathedral and Abbey Churches* that was critical of restorers such as Scott, prompting a debate that led to the formation of the Society for the Protection of Ancient Buildings whose work continues to this day. Nevertheless the external appearance of the cathedral now owes much to Scott.

REMEMBER BECKET
The remains of a bishop's consistory court can be found beneath the south-west tower of Chester Cathedral. Until the nineteenth century this court exercised jurisdiction in matrimonial cases, a relic of the rival law systems that had so exercised Henry II and Thomas à Becket (see 'Saints and sinners'). These courts are now concerned only with the granting of faculties – permission to make changes to church premises

and certain disciplinary matters concerning priests. In the 1930s Chester's consistory court heard its last disputed case, regarding the supposed attempted suicide of a priest, as suicide was then still a crime. Becket would have felt at home there.

CHICHESTER CATHEDRAL

Source of anxiety
A troublesome spire and other architectural wonders

Chichester has been the seat of a bishop since 1075 when the see was transferred from nearby Selsey, and it has had a cathedral since 1108. Like virtually all cathedrals it was extended and embellished over the centuries, the fine spire being added to the structure in the fourteenth century. However this spire was to become the source of much anxiety over the following centuries, receiving the attention of two eminent architects before it attained a reasonably stable condition.

In the seventeenth century it was strengthened by Sir Christopher Wren (see 'A bold but fortunate choice') then survived a severe lightning strike in 1721. However it collapsed in 1861 and was rebuilt, slightly taller, by Sir George Gilbert Scott (see 'An architectural dynasty'), with Queen Victoria contributing to the rebuilding cost. The queen may have seen the cathedral spire as she made her way to her house at Osborne on the Isle of Wight, since the spire of Chichester Cathedral is the only one visible from the sea in Britain – although many may be seen from rivers.

In addition Chichester is unique in having double aisles on each side of the nave, a common feature in France but not in England. And in having a bell tower in a separate building like an Italian campanile, in this case built separately because of the unfortunate tendency of towers to collapse.

The cathedral also contains the remains of a Roman mosaic pavement – indeed the area is so rich in Roman remains that it was clearly a major administrative centre during the Roman occupation of Britain. In the 1960s excavations for a water pipe at nearby Fishbourne revealed the largest Roman palace in Britain – this dates from the first century AD and has the finest Roman mosaics ever discovered in Britain.

Chichester's bell tower

COVENTRY CATHEDRAL

A tale of three cathedrals
The rise and fall of Coventry Cathedral

In 1095 William the Conqueror nominated his chaplain, Robert de Limesey, to the post of Bishop of Coventry. The see was also based at Lichfield, which did not have a cathedral at that time, and the bishop used St Mary's Priory Church at Coventry as his cathedral – no trace of this first church now remains apart from a few ruins.

The priory at Coventry had been endowed in 1043 by Earl Leofric of Mercia and his wife Lady Godiva (died 1080), who was a pious woman associated with a number of religious foundations. Sadly the account of her naked ride through Coventry to shame her husband into reducing the taxes he was levying on his unfortunate vassals, seen only by 'Peeping Tom', which first appears 150 years after the supposed event, has little evidence to support it. Lady

Epstein's St Michael and the Devil

Godiva survived the Norman Conquest and continued to be a major Anglo-Saxon landowner after her husband's death, dying before the Domesday Book was compiled in 1086. When the priory church at Coventry was surrendered to Henry VIII, Coventry lost its first cathedral and its bishop.

The second cathedral was the parish church of St Michael, which became Coventry Cathedral when the diocese and the bishop were re-instated in 1918. Sadly, it is largely remembered for having been destroyed on the night of 14 November 1940 after being a cathedral for only 22 years. It was during one of the most infamous air raids of the Blitz, which left the centre of Coventry, including the cathedral, in ruins and the city an icon of all that was most destructive about twentieth-century warfare. The tower, part of the outer wall and the spire – still the tallest structure in Coventry – survived the raid and were left standing. The words 'Father Forgive' have subsequently been inscribed on one of its charred walls.

On 25 May 1962 the third Coventry Cathedral was consecrated, lying beside the ruins of the old one. Architect Basil Spence designed the new St Michael's Cathedral – his work being chosen from among 200 entries – and the building also incorporated the work of a number of leading British artists: Graham Sutherland designed a tapestry of Christ in Majesty, which at the time was the largest in existence; John Piper designed the Baptistery window; Jacob Epstein created the bronze figure of St Michael triumphing over the devil, which is on the external wall of the cathedral; and Benjamin Britten's *War Requiem*, commissioned for the occasion, received its premiere a few days after the consecration ceremony.

CROSS OF NAILS
*A charred cross was formed from timbers gathered from the ruins of the bombed Coventry Cathedral and a cross of nails was made from nails retrieved from the destroyed roof timbers. The latter now sits in the centre of the altar cross and others, also made from the old cathedral's nails, have been presented to over a hundred centres throughout the world as a symbol of reconciliation. One of them is in the Kaiser Wilhelm Memorial Church in Berlin, itself ruined by bombing late in World War II. One of the crosses was on HMS **Coventry** when she was sunk during the Falklands war – it was later retrieved by divers and is now carried on HMS **Diamond** instead.*

ST DAVIDS CATHEDRAL

Place of pilgrimage
Three visits to St Davids equals one to Jerusalem

The little community of St Davids, founded as a monastery as early as 589 by St David, patron saint of Wales and Abbot of Menevia – now a Roman Catholic diocese based at Swansea – was extremely unfortunate in its location. Between 645 and 1097

St David, the patron saint of Wales

its position on the western extremity of Wales made it an attractive target for any passing marauders – Viking, Irish or plain pirate. Many of the bishops were murdered, including Bishop Abraham as late as 1080, the stone marking his grave being beautifully carved with Celtic symbols. Despite its vulnerability, its reputation was such that King Alfred (849–99) called upon the monks of St Davids to assist him in reviving the intellectual life of Wessex, following his defeat of the Viking invaders.

As late as 1089 the shrine of St David was stripped of its treasures. However in 1115 Henry I of England, then ruling the area, began to build a new cathedral and appointed a Norman named Bernard as the bishop. Bernard shrewdly persuaded the Pope to make St Davids a place of pilgrimage, thus Calixtus II declared 'Two pilgrimages to St Davids is equal to one to Rome and three pilgrimages equal to one to Jerusalem'. St Davids, although remote by most medieval standards, was more accessible to the British than either Rome or Jerusalem. This meant that the papal

decree must have greatly helped the flow of pilgrims and the money they brought, so it is not surprising that the cathedral was quickly completed and consecrated in 1131.

The present Norman design dates mostly from the bishopric of Peter de Leia, starting in 1181, with a major addition during the bishopric of Edward Vaughan between 1509 and 1522 when the Trinity Chapel was built with its fine fan vaulting typical of the Tudor period. The development of the cathedral during this period may owe much to the favour of Henry VII, whose father Edmund Tudor came from Pembrokeshire and whose body was removed to the cathedral in 1540.

'A ruinous state'
The rise of nonconformist churches in Wales

By the late nineteenth century St Davids Cathedral had fallen into a poor state, a contemporary account telling us that: 'At present its appearance is that of a poor village, the houses, excepting those of the clergy, being in a ruinous state' – and in 1888 St Davids even lost its city status!

The reason for this is that during the nineteenth century the number of Welsh people attending nonconformist churches increased to a level at which the privileged position of the established church in Wales became a source of grievance. This church with its bishops was a branch of the Church of England and therefore in a position to collect tithes (taxes on property) from the increasingly estranged nonconformist population. Grievances over payment of tithes had prompted the Rebecca Riots in Wales between 1842 and 1843. Tithes were effectively abolished in 1936 but in the meantime the Welsh Church Act of 1914 disestablished the church in Wales.

Nevertheless in the 1870s the cathedral was extensively refurbished by George Gilbert Scott (see 'An architectural dynasty'), and over a century later, in 1995, Elizabeth II restored city status to St Davids. In addition there was a major refurbishment of the cathedral from the 1950s onwards, with new bells presented by the American Friends

of St Davids Cathedral and a major refurbishment of the cathedral's fabric.

DURHAM CATHEDRAL

Follow that cow!
St Cuthbert finds a final resting place

Uniquely among English cathedrals, Durham Cathedral began its life as a shrine that contained the remains of St Cuthbert. He had been the Bishop of Lindisfarne and after his death in 687 his shrine on the island attracted many pilgrims. However Lindisfarne, or Holy Island, became the victim of the first Viking raid in 793 – after further raids the monks abandoned the site in search of a safer one, taking with them Cuthbert's remains.

Legend insists that the monks followed two dairymaids who were searching for a lost dun (brown) cow. They eventually alighted on a lofty site on a sharp bend in the River Wear, at which point Cuthbert's shrine became immovable. Perhaps the monks were just tired after carrying him up the hill? But in any case, to this day the road leading to the hilltop where the cathedral and castle sit is called Dun Cow Lane.

In its new location Cuthbert's shrine became a place of pilgrimage. When the Normans arrived, seeking a suitable centre from which to administer their new kingdom, they chose the hilltop site and replaced the shrine's small church with a magnificent cathedral for their Prince Bishop (see 'Castle 'gainst the Scot').

NO ORDINARY CATHEDRAL
If there is such a thing as an 'ordinary' cathedral then Durham is definitely not it. Along with its castle, it shares with Canterbury the distinction of having been declared a World Heritage Site by UNESCO, which reported in 1986 that the cathedral was the largest and most perfect monument of Norman style architecture in England. During its existence the cathedral has been or is: a shrine, a sanctuary, a fortification, a film set and a prison where many died. And for a long time the Bishop of Durham was more a warrior than a churchman.

'Castle 'gainst the Scot'
Bishops buckle on their swords

King Canute was among the early pilgrims to visit the shrine of St Cuthbert that the Lindisfarne monks had established at Durham (see 'Follow that cow!'). However after the Norman Conquest William I chose Durham as a site for the administration of the north of his new kingdom and elevated the White Church, which had previously housed St Cuthbert's shrine, to cathedral status. He appointed the first bishop, William of Calais, as his Prince Bishop Palatine, the secular as well as religious governor with responsibility for keeping his troublesome northern subjects in order and protecting his kingdom from the Scots. Perhaps one of those Scots, Sir Walter Scott, best expresses the unique character of the cathedral as castle, church and place of scholarship in his poem 'Harold the Dauntless', which tells of Saxon and Viking conflicts in County Durham:

Grey towers of Durham
Yet well I love thy mixed
   and massive piles
Half church of God, half
   castle 'gainst the Scot
And long to roam those
   venerable aisles
With records stored of deeds long
   since forgot.

Although Scott's poem long predates the construction of the Great Northern Railway, there is no better way of seeing what he meant in his poem than by viewing this majestic cathedral that towers over the sharp bend in the River Wear from the East Coast Railway Line, as it wends its way north towards Newcastle and Edinburgh. Durham was in effect the capital of the north of England, which in the opinion of its citizens it remains, with the bishop as the representative of the king.

To begin with all went well with the Scottish neighbours. Tactfully, William of Calais invited Malcolm, King of Scotland – and slayer of the much maligned Macbeth – to attend the ceremony when the foundation stone for a new cathedral was laid in 1093. The structure was completed by 1135, a fine example of Norman architecture unsurpassed anywhere in the world with its massive stone columns decorated with chevrons and squares surmounted by magnificent dogtooth arches.

Durham Cathedral, 'Half castle 'gainst the Scot'

This failed to impress the Scots for long and the bishops of Durham were frequently called upon to put away their mitres and buckle on their swords. This was perhaps most notable at the Battle of Flodden in 1513 when an invading Scottish army was put to flight, their king and much of their nobility having been killed by the warrior bishop's army.

The Bishop of Durham remained a secular as well as religious official for almost 800 years, until 1836 when Bishop William Van Mildert, the great-grandson of a Dutch merchant, gave up his princely status and became a plain bishop. But to this day the Bishop of Durham is the fourth bishop in precedence in the Church of England behind the archbishops of Canterbury and York, and the Bishop of London. And he retains the privilege of standing at the right hand of the monarch at the coronation ceremony.

DURHAM UNIVERSITY
Founded in 1837 and the first university in the north of England, Durham University disputes the title of being the third oldest university in England with University College London. William Van Mildert was one of the founders of the University of Durham, which has over 60 listed buildings that range from the eleventh-century castle to an Art Deco chapel dating from the 1930s. Henry VIII and Oliver Cromwell both planned to found a university at Durham but were frustrated by the jealousy and intransigence of Oxford and Cambridge.

Memorials
And the site of a mass grave

Even the bishop's princely status at the time (see 'Castle 'gainst the Scot') could not defend the shrine of Cuthbert at Durham Cathedral from the depredations of Henry VIII, who ordered that it be destroyed during the dissolution of the monasteries. However the saint's body was exhumed, and being found well preserved it was buried beneath a stone slab that remains in the cathedral and continues to attract visitors. Cuthbert's remains have been joined by the remains of the

Venerable Bede (673–735), a monk of Jarrow who is regarded as the father of English historical writing for his *Ecclesiastical History of the English People* and his translations into Anglo-Saxon of early Latin and Greek texts. Henry VIII's henchmen also looted his tomb but Bede's remains were re-interred in the cathedral, where they remain. Bede is unique among Englishmen in having been declared a Doctor of the Church by the Pope in 1899.

However it is not only venerable churchmen who are remembered in the cathedral. On the second Saturday of July each year the Big Meeting is held in Durham. Better known as the Durham Miners' Gala, this is a celebration of the mining industry in the county. The first meeting was in 1871 and is still held each year, attended by about 50,000 people, despite the fact that mining in the county has ceased. The procession of banners belonging to collieries long since closed, each accompanied by a brass band, makes its way to the racecourse to hear political speeches. In the afternoon a service is held in the cathedral to celebrate the

contribution of mining to the life and wellbeing of the City and County of Durham – attendance at the Durham Miners' Gala is a rite of passage for any politician who aspires to left-wing credentials. In addition the sacrifices made by miners are remembered in one of the cathedral's many memorials.

There are other even sadder memorials. Following the Battle of Dunbar in September 1650, when Oliver Cromwell defeated a Scottish army who had risen on behalf of the future King Charles II, Durham Cathedral was used as a prison to hold about 3,000 Scottish prisoners of war. They existed without adequate food, water or heat in cold weather, using much of the cathedral's furniture as firewood. About half of them died, the remaining ones being either sentenced to transportation for America or force-marched to East Anglia to work on draining the fens. In 1946 a mass grave of Scots was discovered during work to install a new central heating system in the cathedral and in 2010 an agreement was made to install a memorial to the victims in the chapel of St Margaret of Scotland within the cathedral.

SANCTUARY KNOCKER

Durham Cathedral is unusual in retaining a Sanctuary Knocker, which a criminal in flight could use to seek entry to the cathedral as a refuge from his pursuers. Once admitted he would be required to wear a plain black garment with the yellow cross of St Cuthbert on the left breast, he would be fed a plain diet of bread and water, and would be given 37 days to leave England for ever via the Palatine Port of Hartlepool. He would leave on foot, carrying a cross and accompanied by parish

Durham's Sanctuary Knocker

constables throughout his journey before being put on a vessel for the continent. If, when walking to the port, he strayed from the highway, or if he ever returned to England again, he would be put to death. The original knocker is in the cathedral museum and the one on the door, with its lion head, is a bronze replica.

ELY CATHEDRAL

Ship of the Fens
On the island of eels

Ely Cathedral is by far the most conspicuous feature of the Fenland north of Cambridge. It rises high above the watery landscape and is particularly striking when seen from the railway line, which runs from the East Coast main line to its junction at Ely. Known as the Ship of the Fens, the cathedral sits on what is still known as the Isle of Ely, although since the drainage works of the seventeenth century it is no longer as isolated as it was in the period after the Norman Conquest when it provided a refuge for Hereward the Wake in his rebellion. In Old English the Isle of Ely means island of eels, these long being a staple food harvested from the surrounding peat-brown streams and for many years taken in water-filled barrels to London markets for sale. Some are still caught to this day by traditional methods and served as a delicacy.

The construction of the present cathedral, initially built as an abbey, was begun in 1083 under the Norman Abbot Simeon who was then 90 years old and the brother of Walkelin who, as Bishop of Winchester, was engaged in building the Norman cathedral in that city (see 'Walkelin's structure'). The Norman abbey was built of limestone from Peterborough Abbey's quarries at Barnack, purchased by Ely for the price of 8,000 eels per year. When Simeon died in 1093, probably at the age of 100, his work was continued by his successors, Abbot Richard and later, in 1107, by Abbot Hervey

The Ship of the Fens

de Breton, a third Norman. After a long campaign Breton became the first Bishop of Ely in 1109 when the diocese was carved out of the huge diocese of Lincoln – Ely Abbey thus became a cathedral.

There had been an earlier abbey at Ely, founded in 672 by St Etheldreda, daughter of King Anna of East Anglia. After destructive raids by Vikings this older abbey was rebuilt close to the later site of the Norman building. The establishment of the diocese and its cathedral prompted Bishop Hervey to place a shrine to St Etheldreda with its relics in the new building, where they remained. Construction of the cathedral continued for almost three centuries thereafter, incorporating Early English and decorated Gothic styles in its design. When St Etheldreda's relics and shrine were moved to a new site near the high altar, the cathedral was re-consecrated in the presence of Henry III (1207– 72) and his son, the future Edward I.

HEREWARD THE WAKE

Hereward (eleventh century) was a Saxon who led resistance to the Normans in the Fenland of East Anglia and about whom Charles Kingsley wrote a popular novel. Although there are conflicting accounts of his activities – a particularly improbable one has him as the son of Lady Godiva (see 'A tale of three cathedrals') – there is sound evidence for his existence. He was probably born in Lincolnshire and outlawed by Edward the Confessor in 1054, returning to England after the Norman Conquest to take up arms against the Normans who had confiscated his family's lands. He sacked Peterborough Abbey, retreated to a stronghold on the Isle of Ely that was accessible only across marshy ground, and eventually fled into exile when the Normans seized Ely after building a causeway from the small settlement of Aldreth. This causeway, with a bridge across the River Ouse, may still be seen today.

Distinctive features
The Lady Chapel and lantern

In 1321 construction of Ely Cathedral's huge and dramatic Lady Chapel, the largest in

Ely's lantern

England, was begun to the north of the high altar. It is one of the most distinctive features of the cathedral and would alone make a magnificent church. However its creation was probably responsible for the existence of a unique feature for which the cathedral is most famous – the lantern.

Shortly after building began on the Lady Chapel, the Norman crossing tower collapsed, probably as the excavation for the foundations of

the chapel had weakened its own foundations. Instead of replacing the tower the stonemason, Alan de Walsingham, took the opportunity to design a unique octagonal tower in its place with timber vaulting supporting a glazed timber lantern, also octagonal. No other cathedral has anything like it.

Vandals descend
Years of neglect and decay

In 1539 Thomas Cromwell's commissioners took possession of the monastery at Ely and the last prior, Robert Steward, became the dean of the cathedral, upon which more than the usual destruction was then wrought. Anglo-Saxon shrines were destroyed, stained glass was smashed, and statues were either broken up or decapitated. Many of these statues remain in that condition, especially in the Lady Chapel, a testament to the vengeful iconoclasm of the Tudor vandals. The monastic buildings, emptied of monks, were converted for use as a grammar school, which continues to flourish to this day.

It may be because of this destruction that the cathedral escaped fairly lightly from the attention of Parliamentary forces during the English Civil War (1642–51). East Anglia largely supported Parliament during the conflict, although this fact alone did not spare nearby Cambridge. But at Ely most of the destruction had already been done by the Tudors so there wasn't much left to offend the Puritans. Even so, Parliament suggested that the remaining buildings be demolished and the materials sold to pay for 'relief of sick and maimed soldiers, widows and children'.

Fortunately the buildings were simply neglected and left to decay for a century. The fact that the Parliamentary orders were never carried out may owe something to the fact that Oliver Cromwell, Member of Parliament for Cambridge, lived in Ely (where his house may still be visited) and wished to protect it. However it did not prevent Cromwell from putting the Bishop of Ely, Matthew Wren, in the Tower of London in 1642 where he remained for 18 years.

In the following centuries the cathedral was carefully restored by several architects, including the ubiquitous Sir George Gilbert Scott (see 'An architectural dynasty') – it was his first major commission. One was less fortunate: George Basevi, architect of much of Belgravia and of Cambridge's Fitzwilliam Museum, fell to his death while inspecting one of the towers and is buried in the cathedral.

Cambridge University falls within the diocese of Ely and it is therefore interesting to discover that many figures associated with the university are buried within it. Hugh de Balsham, Bishop of Ely from 1256 to 1286, was the founder of Cambridge's first college, Peterhouse. John Alcock, Bishop of Ely, Lord Chancellor of England and founder of Jesus College, is buried in his own chantry chapel – the Jesus College crest, consisting of three cockerels, commemorates the name of its founder there.

ELY ON FILM AND AN ALBUM COVER
Ely Cathedral has been used as a location for several major

films. **Elizabeth: The Golden Age**, *starring Cate Blanchett as Elizabeth I, was filmed there in 2006. In 2007* **The Other Boleyn Girl** *followed, an account of the life of Anne Boleyn's sister Mary that featured future stars such as* **Eddie Redmayne and Benedict Cumberbatch.** *In November 2009 the cathedral became Westminster Abbey for* **The King's Speech,** *which starred Colin Firth as King George VI and Geoffrey Rush as the king's speech therapist, Lionel Logue. More improbably, the cathedral featured on the cover of Pink Floyd's 1994 album* **The Division Bell.**

EXETER CATHEDRAL

An elephant with horse's hooves
And the longest vaulted ceiling in England

In 1050 the Bishop of Devon and Cornwall decided to move his seat to Exeter, which was surrounded by its Roman wall (much of which may still be seen) and therefore better protected from raiders than the smaller town of Crediton in which he had previously been based. A Saxon minster served as a temporary cathedral until William I's nephew, Warelwast, was appointed bishop in 1107 and began to build a fine cathedral in the Norman style, as was the Norman habit.

Much of this original cathedral remains although the cathedral is better known for its later additions that continued into the fifteenth century, which left it with the longest vaulted ceiling in England. It survived the Tudor despoilers better than many cathedrals because it had never been attached to a monastery, so today it is one of a handful of churches in the West Country to contain an astronomical clock. Dating from about 1484, this registers the position of the sun in the sky and the phases of the moon.

The cathedral's misericords, in turn dating from the thirteenth century, are outnumbered only by those of Wells yet are still unique in having all survived the attentions of the

Exeter Cathedral

iconoclasts of later centuries. Besides foliage and domestic animals, these misericords feature a shot putter, a lion and a mermaid, as well as an elephant – the first wooden carving of this animal ever seen in England, following the gift of an elephant to Henry III by Louis IX of France in 1253. The carver was either unobservant or working from an inaccurate picture – possibly that of Matthew Paris (1200–59 – see 'Off with his head!') – since he gave the elephant horses' hooves!

'Knock out their teeth'
Exeter becomes the first victim of the Baedeker Raids

Sadly, Exeter Cathedral is remembered as the first victim of the so-called Baedeker Raids of World War II. These came about because in March 1942 the Royal Air Force launched its first mass bombing of a German city when it attacked the port of Lubeck, which lies in the Schleswig-Holstein region at the western edge of the Baltic Sea.

Port cities were chosen because at night the city lights contrasted with the dark sea, enabling the bombers to find their targets more easily than they could over land in the days of primitive navigational equipment.

The resulting destruction visited on the ancient historic port and its wooden buildings alarmed and outraged the Nazi leaders. Joseph Goebbels (1898–1945) announced that the Luftwaffe would take time off from its attack on the crumbling Russian armies to attack England: 'Cultural centres, health resorts and civilian centres must be attacked. There is no other way of bringing the English to their senses. They belong to a class of human beings with whom you can only talk after you have knocked out their teeth'. One of his officials added, 'We shall go out and bomb every building in Britain marked with three stars in the Baedeker Guide', the *Baedeker Guides* being the equivalent of the later *Blue Guides* to European cities.

Thus it happened that Exeter, a city of little military or strategic importance, was the first victim of the Baedeker Raids on the night of 23–24 April 1942. A later raid on 4 May of the same year inflicted some damage on the cathedral, although the earlier one had prompted the removal of some of the more vulnerable treasures from the building, including a number of ancient manuscripts.

However the damage was made good after the war. On 7 March 1951 a Festival of Rugby was held in Exeter to raise money for the restoration of the cathedral, the highlight being a match between Exeter and the Oxford University Rugby XV that contained several international players. Oxford won by six points to nil, an indignant local reporter claiming that this was because Exeter's only penalty kicker was injured. However the visitors were evidently forgiven because a carving of an Oxford player was included as a corbel in the restored St James' Chapel, where he may still be seen opposite a carving of George Down, the stonemason who restored much of the stonework.

ST GILES' CATHEDRAL, EDINBURGH

Protestant firebrand
John Knox's tenure at St Giles'

St Giles' Cathedral in Edinburgh, or to give it its correct (and much older) name, the High Kirk of Edinburgh, is not strictly a cathedral at all – like all cathedrals belonging to the Church of Scotland, it lacks a bishop. Indeed it was only a cathedral complete with a bishop for two short periods during the civil wars of the 1640s between Charles I and Parliament, while the British Isles were ravaged by savage and often fatal conflicts regarding the finer points of the Christian faith. Yet St Giles' – which takes its name from the patron saint of the city, a seventh-century hermit whose connection with Edinburgh is about as great as that of St Andrew with Scotland – earns its place here because of its historic place in those controversies in which it played a central, spectacular and violent part.

The cathedral occupies a prominent site on Edinburgh's Royal Mile, which runs from Edinburgh Castle to the Royal Palace of Holyrood, and the building's famous crown steeple makes it even more conspicuous. Most of the structure dates from the fourteenth century, but it entered upon its most famous period when the firebrand ultra-Protestant preacher John Knox became its minister in 1559. Tact and diplomacy were not qualities that came naturally to Knox: in 1558, during a period of exile in Geneva and following the marriage of Mary Stewart (later Queen of Scots) to the Catholic dauphin, heir to the French throne, Knox had written a pamphlet entitled *The First Blast of the Trumpet against the Monstrous Regiment of Women*. In it he declared 'how abominable before God is the Empire or Rule of a wicked woman, yea a traitresse and bastard'.

Elizabeth I became Queen of England the same year and Knox hinted that he would like to be offered a position in the Church of England. When it was suggested that his pamphlet had not strengthened his claims, he replied that he was not 'minded to retreat or call back any principal point or proposition of the same'. This was as near as one got to an apology from Knox, so it may come as no surprise that Elizabeth was unimpressed, which meant that St Giles' was blessed with his services instead. Knox was buried in the cathedral's churchyard that eventually became a car park for the High Court of Scotland, where a stone set in the tarmac marks the position of his grave.

In 1633 Charles I, assisted by William Laud, Archbishop of

St Giles' crown steeple

Canterbury, began his misguided attempt to oblige the reluctant and distinctly Protestant Scots to adopt the Anglican Book of Common Prayer. As the Dean of St Giles', John Hannah, began to read from the Book on Sunday 23 July 1637, a market trader named Jenny Geddes hurled her stool at his head, provoking riots that led to the start of the civil wars that were to end with the beheading of Charles I in 1649. This experiment with the Anglican rite did not last long. The bishops disappeared along with James II of England (VII of Scotland) in 1689 and Elders, who are elected by congregations, and ministers – all collectively known as presbyters – now govern the Church of Scotland.

BAGPIPE-PLAYING ANGEL

St Giles', along with other Presbyterian churches, is far less elaborately decorated than English cathedrals. However its Thistle Chapel, which is dedicated to the Order of the Thistle, does contain some finely carved vaulting and a figure of an angel playing the bagpipes. The Thistle, Scotland's premier order of chivalry, had been founded by Scotland's unfortunate James VII and consists of the monarch and 16 knights.

GLASGOW CATHEDRAL

A saint with two names
And a cathedral without a bishop

Glasgow Cathedral

The present Glasgow Cathedral dates from the late twelfth century and is in the Scottish Gothic style. However it is built on the site of an earlier church of St Mungo, also known as St Kentigern, the patron saint of Glasgow, who died in 614 and whose tomb is in the crypt of the cathedral.

St Mungo's shrine became a site of great pilgrimage until the Reformation, when divines such as John Knox expressed their disapproval of such practices. Yet St Mungo's tomb, unlike those of many saints in England, survived the attentions of the reformers and may still be seen.

Moreover St Mungo's figure appears in the Glasgow City Crest together with a representation of four miracles attributed to him – he restored a robin to life, relit a fire with a hazel branch, brought a bell from Rome and caught a fish that contained a lost ring. These miracles are expressed in verse as follows:

Here is the bird that never flew
Here is the tree that never grew
Here is the bell that never rang
Here is the fish that never swam

Most unusually the cathedral has a medieval rood screen, a representation of the crucifixion –

the great majority were destroyed by reformers. However it does not have a bishop. The bishopric was abolished in 1690, so Glasgow Cathedral is in the strange position of being a cathedral without a bishop.

PROMOTING SCIENCE

In the fifteenth century Scotland had only one university, St Andrews, which was founded in 1413. In 1451 Glasgow University became the second Scottish university, founded by Bishop William Turnbull of Glasgow Cathedral. For the first two centuries of its existence the Bishop of Glasgow was ex officio Chancellor of the University, a learning establishment that was to produce such celebrated alumni of science as Lord Lister, a pioneer of antiseptic surgery, James Watt, an inventor of steam engines, and Lord Kelvin, the physicist.

The cathedral was less successful in bringing peace than it was in promoting science. In 1502 King James IV of Scotland ratified the Treaty of Perpetual Peace with England but this didn't last – 11 years later he marched into England at the head of an invading army. James was defeated and killed at Flodden by an army led by the Bishop of Durham and Henry VIII's wife, Catherine of Aragon – much of Scotland's nobility also lay dead on the battlefield. So much for Perpetual Peace!

GLASTONBURY ABBEY

Place of legends
The wealthy abbey on a tor

====

Glastonbury in Somerset is a place of legends. Mostly, it must be said, this is down to the ingenuity of the abbey's medieval monks in 'discovering' evidence that linked the site not only to King Arthur, but also to Joseph of Arimathea, who had provided the tomb in Jerusalem from which Christ rose from the dead.

The hilltop site itself on which Glastonbury Abbey is located is known as Glastonbury Tor, a 'tor' meaning a bare hilltop in Old English. In the Dark Ages this tor was even more surrounded by water than it is now and it is genuinely ancient, with evidence of Christian worship from the early seventh century, even before the Anglo-Saxons arrived to disturb the peace of the Celtic tribes, or ancient Britons.

After Alfred the Great had disposed of the usual Viking difficulties, Glastonbury became a prosperous Benedictine house under St Dunstan, who eventually became Archbishop of Canterbury in 960. A measure of the abbey's wealth is that at this time it built its own canal, a mile in length, to link the abbey with the River Brue for the transport of building materials, wine, fish and other produce.

According to the Domesday Book, in 1086 Glastonbury was the wealthiest monastery in England. Half a century later the abbey commissioned the normally reputable historian William of Malmesbury to write an account of its history with the purpose of establishing the abbey's ascendancy over rivals such as Westminster and a link with King Arthur and his knights. This was to prove useful when the abbey ran into hard times.

Timely discovery
The tombs of Arthur and Guinevere

Hard times arrived for Glastonbury Abbey in 1184 when a fire destroyed the buildings. Money was needed, so it was very convenient that the tombs of King Arthur and his Queen Guinevere were 'discovered' beneath a stone in 1191. According to a contemporary account by Geraldus Cambrensis (c. 1146–1223), known

A royal grave?

as Gerald of Wales, this stone bore the inscription in Latin: 'Here lies interred the famous King Arthur on the Isle of Avalon'.

Geraldus regarded this as evidence that Arthur was dead, a discovery that would dispense with tales that he was sleeping, awaiting a call to drive out the Saxon and Norman invaders. Geraldus went on to write: 'Many tales are told and many legends have been invented about King Arthur and his mysterious ending. In their stupidity the British [ie Celts, like himself] maintain that he is still alive… The fairy tales have been snuffed out.' In 1278 Edward I and

Queen Eleanor attended the reburial of the royal couple and the site of their supposed tomb may still be seen.

Pilgrimages resumed
Boosted by Joseph of Arimathea and rock music

As Glastonbury Abbey's fortunes recovered (see 'Timely discovery') the pilgrimages resumed, later boosted by the legend that Joseph of Arimathea had visited the site and planted the Glastonbury thorn – a type of hawthorn that unusually flowers twice a year, once in spring and again in winter. The

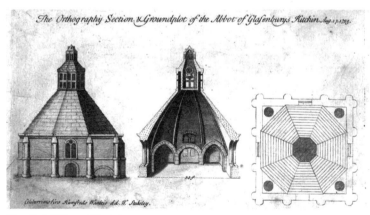

The abbot's kitchen at Glastonbury

wealth of the abbey was restored and the rebuilding was completed that has left us with a very fine abbot's kitchen, possibly the best in Europe, which was later used as a Quaker meeting house. The Abbot's Fish House on the River Brue was also completed where the monastery's pike, tench, roach and eels were prepared and salted, fish being served on Fridays, fast days and during Lent – it remains to this day the only surviving monastic fish house in the UK.

The abbey succumbed to Thomas Cromwell's commissioners in 1539, Abbot Richard Whiting being executed by the grotesque method of being hung, drawn and quartered along with two of his monks on Glastonbury Tor because he had offended the commissioners by resisting their attempts to suppress the abbey. He had to wait until 1895 to be beatified by the Pope as a Catholic martyr. The monastery and its extensive lands passed into the possession of the Thynne family who became Marquesses of Bath, and it was finally purchased in the twentieth century by the diocese of Bath and Wells.

Glastonbury is now perhaps best known for its music festival that in fact takes place at nearby Pilton Farm. Yet it remains a place of pilgrimage from which each year a branch of the winter budding Glastonbury thorn is sent to Queen Elizabeth II. Perhaps she puts it on her Christmas tree?

GLOUCESTER CATHEDRAL

Origins of Domesday
*With golf and football
in the cathedral*

The *Anglo-Saxon Chronicle*, an early record of English history originally commissioned by Alfred the Great, records how William the Conqueror (1027–87) spent Christmas in the nineteenth year of his reign of England: 'While spending the Christmas time of 1085 in Gloucester, William had deep speech with his counsellors and sent men all over England to each shire to find out what or how much each landholder had in land and livestock and what it was worth.' From this process began the compilation of the Domesday Book in 1086, perhaps an even more important historical record than the *Anglo-Saxon Chronicle* itself, which was used for taxation and judging land disputes over the centuries that followed. It remains to this day an important source document for medieval historians.

At the time of William's visit to the establishment, Gloucester Cathedral was an abbey church, standing by the River Severn, which had been founded in around 678 by Osric, a prince of the kingdom of the Hwicce (see 'Throne in a spa'). The Norman church that William visited, of which much remains, was later extended and embellished in the Perpendicular Gothic style, with soaring narrow pillars that supported the first fan vaults ever built. These were constructed in the building's cloisters by a stonemason named Thomas de Cambridge between 1351 and 1377.

In 1540 the Benedictine monastery that the church had served was dissolved by Henry VIII and the abbey became instead the Cathedral of the Holy and Undivided Trinity. The abbey was not despoiled by the

Gloucester's fan vaulted cloisters

Tudors as some were and one of the stained glass windows that survives, dating from about 1350, shows a golfer – the earliest on record.

In the south transept the cathedral's fine stonework includes a carving of a young man falling, thought either to represent a stonemason falling to his death while working on the cathedral, perhaps as a memorial or tribute to his work, or a miraculous escape from a fatal fall. There is also a carved image of people who appear to be playing football, the first such image of what became the world's most popular game. The East Window, also known as the Crecy Window because it features the family crests of two local knights who fought at the Battle of Crecy in 1346, was at the time of its installation in the 1350s the largest window in the world and much of its early glass survived later vandals.

MADE IN ENGLAND

Fan vaulting is a peculiarly English architectural style that largely flourished during the Tudor period, very rarely seen beyond these shores. Besides Gloucester Cathedral, other examples are at Sherborne Abbey, St George's Chapel at Windsor and the Lady Chapel built by Henry VII, also known as the Royal Air Force Chapel, at Westminster Abbey. The world's largest fan vault was built in King's College Chapel at Cambridge almost two centuries later than the one at Gloucester – weighing 1,000 tons, it appears to defy gravity.

Gloucester's extravagant medieval stonework has made it very attractive to producers of films and television programmes. Three of the Harry Potter films used it as a location and in 2008 an episode of **Doctor Who** *was filmed there. More recently the cathedral was used as the court of Henry VIII in the BBC television series* **Wolf Hall**, *based on Hilary Mantel's account of Thomas Cromwell's career.*

What became of Edward II?
A coronation, an execution and a mystery

The abbey church on the site of what is now Gloucester Cathedral was the scene of one coronation, hastily arranged in 1216 after the sudden death of King John. His son Prince Henry was crowned Henry III on 28 October 1216 only nine days after the death of his father, the haste due to anxiety among his nobles to ensure that there was no disputed succession. Henry was crowned in the abbey church where his distant relative, Robert Curthose, was buried in 1134. Robert had been the eldest son of William the Conqueror. On his father's death, he became Duke of Normandy while his younger brothers, William then Henry, became Kings of England. Robert had attempted to seize the kingdom from Henry but was defeated and imprisoned at Cardiff Castle, living into his 80s before dying in 1134 and being buried at Gloucester.

Edward II, according to history,

died in 1327 after being deposed by his wife, Queen Isabella, with the help of her lover Roger Mortimer and many of Edward's barons who were repelled by the favouritism that Edward had shown to men who were also suspected of being his lovers. Edward was certainly an unpopular and incompetent king whose disastrous defeat at Bannockburn in 1314 was only the most conspicuous embarrassment of his disastrous reign. According to the official account, Edward was put to death in Berkeley Castle by a method possibly involving a hot poker, strangling or starvation, the method chosen being designed to ensure that at the time of his burial there were no signs of violence on

Edward II

the royal corpse. He was duly buried in what was to become Gloucester Cathedral in what is possibly the finest of royal tombs, surmounted by an effigy of the dead king in alabaster.

Or was he? By some accounts Edward was spirited away from Berkeley to Corfe in Dorset, and from there to Germany where, according to one account, he was secretly visited by his son and successor Edward III. This son was a much more popular and successful king than his father, wreaking a terrible revenge on Mortimer by executing him in 1330. In the nineteenth century a document was discovered in France, apparently written by an agent of the Pope named Manuel Fieschi, which claimed that Fieschi had found the king living as a hermit in Italy near Milan. These claims were examined in some detail by two accounts written in 2010 that raised significant doubts about the official version of Edward II's controversial death.

Whatever his true fate Edward II, who had been unpopular in his lifetime, was revered after his death and his tomb attracted pilgrims whose offerings helped to pay for

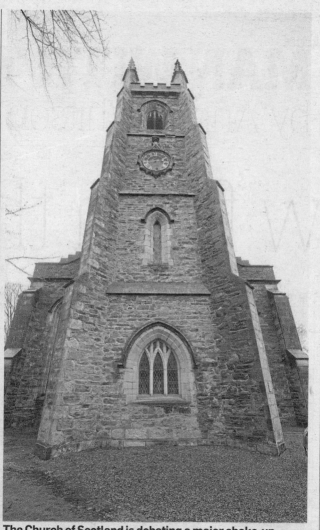

The Church of Scotland is debating a major shake-up.

w from th

r,

k
n

the cloisters with their fan vaults and the reconstruction of the east end of the cathedral, including the choir and the Crecy Window.

UNETHICAL EXPERIMENT

Gloucester Cathedral also contains a statue of Edward Jenner (1749–1823), a local doctor who had observed that milkmaids, famed for their fine complexions, never caught the common, disfiguring and often fatal disease of smallpox. He concluded that the cowpox blisters they had on their hands from milking protected them from the disease, testing his hypothesis first by injecting James Phipps, the eight-year-old son of his gardener, with pus from cowpox then with smallpox itself.

Fortunately for James and for Jenner the child had, as the doctor had supposed, developed an immunity from smallpox. So after much controversy, vaccination was adopted throughout the world and in 1979 the World Health Organization declared that smallpox was an eradicated disease. If Jenner were to conduct such an experiment now

he would be struck off the medical register and possibly gaoled!

HEREFORD CATHEDRAL

The unfortunate fiancé
And a string of controversial bishops

Unusually Hereford Cathedral, besides receiving the common dedication to St Mary, is also dedicated to the memory of a king, in this case St Ethelbert (died 794). Having been betrothed to the daughter of King Offa of Mercia, Ethelbert was then beheaded on Offa's orders. When miracles were reported from the site of the unfortunate fiancé's beheading, a small church was built by a Mercian nobleman called Milfrid close to the banks of the River Wye. This became the seat of a diocese that had been founded in about 676 by a former Bishop of Rochester named Putta and hence became a cathedral. But the establishment had little more luck than Ethelbert, being sacked by a force of Welsh and Irishmen then having to wait for the first Norman bishops before it was rebuilt.

The early Norman bishops were not always noted for their piety and one of the most enterprising, Peter of Aigueblanche, Bishop of Hereford between 1241 and 1268, spent much of his time rebuilding the cathedral using money he had extorted from citizens of Ireland. A stern rebuke from the future King Edward I recalled him to his duties. One of his successors, Thomas de Cantilupe, who was bishop between 1275 and 1282, was more merciful to his flock. Upon learning that a local magnate, Lord Clifford, had stolen cattle from his tenants, he obliged the wretched man to walk barefoot to the high altar of the cathedral where Cantilupe applied the rod to his back. In 1320 the Pope declared Cantilupe a saint on account of the miracles that were reported from his shrine at the cathedral and the fact that he habitually wore a hair shirt. His coat of arms was adopted for the diocese of Hereford.

Later centuries gave the diocese some equally controversial bishops.

In 1848 Dr Renn Hampden was appointed by the Liberal Prime Minister, Lord John Russell. This provoked a good deal of controversy, owing to Hampden's liberal views. He had argued that people who were not Anglicans should be able to attend Oxford University and had thereby drawn upon himself the wrath of both the Dean of Hereford and many of the bishops. In the nineteenth century the cathedral was restored by George Gilbert Scott (see 'An architectural dynasty'), but he was too late to save the cathedral's beautiful chapter house that had been ruined during the English Civil War (1642–51) – in a vain attempt to repel the Parliamentary army besieging the town, the Royalist one had melted down its lead roof to make bullets.

The cathedral was re-opened in 1863 after Scott's restoration. Hampden's fellow bishop, Samuel Wilberforce of Oxford, listened intently for signs of liberalism but reported that Hampden's sermon was 'dull, but thoroughly orthodox'. Wilberforce was not himself a man troubled by self-doubt, writing of his own service that 'I preached evening; great congregation and much interested'. The poor man had obviously recovered from a bruising encounter with Charles Darwin's friend, Thomas Huxley, which had occurred in 1859 – in a public debate on Darwin's *On the Origin of Species* Huxley had humiliated 'Soapy Sam', as Wilberforce was known.

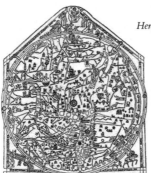

Hereford's Mappa Mundi

'A fortuitous and friendly proposal'
Three cathedrals, three choirs, one festival

In the early eighteenth century the Bishop of Hereford, Philip Bisse, in what appears to have been an act of nepotism, appointed his brother Thomas to the post of Canon Chancellor of Hereford Cathedral. Thomas had previously worked in London and had been greatly impressed by the choral services held at St Paul's in aid of charity. He was an enthusiastic musician, who preached a sermon entitled 'Music the Delight of the Sons of Men'. When he took up his post Thomas Bisse made 'a fortuitous and friendly proposal between a few lovers of harmony and brethren of the correspondent choirs, to commence an anniversary visit…to the improvement of our choirs, the credit of our foundations, the benefit of our cities…to the delight of mankind…'

BOOKS IN CHAINS
Hereford Cathedral is famous for its chained library of over 1,000 extremely valuable ancient manuscript books, including a copy of the Gospels that is at least 1,000 years old. The greatest treasure is the **Mappa Mundi***, a work of the late thirteenth century by a clergyman called Richard de Haldingham and Lafford near Seaford in Lincolnshire. Drawn on a sheet of vellum it shows the earth as round surrounded by the oceans, and marks the cities of Jerusalem, Babylon, Rome and Troy.*

This portentous language marked the beginning of the Three Choirs Festival, which probably began in the year of Bisse's appointment and has been an annual event since 1724. It involves the cathedrals of Hereford, Gloucester and Worcester and takes place in the last week of July. Hereford already had a strong musical tradition thanks to its organist John Bull (c. 1562–1628) who was one of the first composers of music specifically for keyboard instruments and whose name later become identified with distinctive qualities of Englishness. The festival annually rotates between the three cathedrals and has a strong claim to being the oldest classical music festival in the world.

In its early days the festival was dominated by the works of Purcell and Handel, and in the twentieth century it became a showcase for the

Edward Elgar

work of English composers such as Vaughan Williams, Frederick Delius, Gustav Holst, Gerald Finzi, William Walton, Benjamin Britten, Arthur Bliss and, of course, Edward Elgar – one of Worcester's greatest sons. Among the works that received their first performance at the festival were Vaughan Williams's *Fantasia on a Theme by Thomas Tallis*, Haydn's *Creation* and Sir Hubert Parry's *De Profundis*.

LEICESTER CATHEDRAL

King in the car park
Richard III's body is discovered

Richard III (1452–85) is perhaps the most unfortunate of our monarchs. The last of the Plantagenets and monarch for only two years before becoming the last English king to be killed in battle by the army of Henry VII, he then had the much greater misfortune to have his character assassinated by William Shakespeare. In the opening lines of his play *Richard III*, Shakespeare gives Richard, Duke of Gloucester, some of the most memorable but also some of the most self-incriminating lines in literature.

Richard greets the coronation of his elder brother Edward IV thus:

Now is the winter
  of our discontent
Made glorious summer
  by this son of York
And all the clouds that
  lowered upon our house
In the deep bosom of
  the ocean buried.

But later in the same speech he adds:

I am determined to prove a villain
And hate the idle
  pleasure of these days.

Condemned by his own mouth in his opening speech! Shakespeare, of course, was working to an agenda, which was to demonstrate that the grandfather of the playwright's

monarch, Elizabeth I, performed a heroic act in defeating and killing such a blackguard at the Battle of Bosworth in 1485. Later scholars have taken a more benign view of Richard, as one who brought to an end the anarchy of the Wars of the Roses and may not even have connived in the murder of his nephews.

In 2012 archaeologists from the University of Leicester, following a number of neglected historical clues, excavated a car park in Leicester – it was built on the former site of a friary, where some contemporary writers suggested Richard's body had been buried after the battle. Quite soon after the excavation began, a skeleton was discovered with spinal curvature of the kind attributed to Richard in exaggerated form by Shakespeare and others.

In February 2013, following DNA analysis and comparisons with living descendants of Richard's sister, Anne of York, it was announced that the skeleton was indeed that of Richard III. There followed a lengthy argument about where he should be buried. Would it be Leicester, close to where he died? Or would it be York, on the

Richard III at rest

LINCOLN CATHEDRAL

Taller than the Great Pyramid
Until the spire was blown down in a storm

grounds that he was the last king of the House of York? Leicester won the argument and on 26 March 2015 he was reburied in the city's cathedral within an oak coffin made by a direct descendant of Richard's sister. A piece of Yorkshire was included in the burial in the form of a tombstone quarried in Swaledale.

In this way one of England's less well-known cathedrals had its hours in the limelight. It had in fact only been a cathedral since 1927, following the creation of the new diocese of Leicester, although the building itself was a Norman foundation, having previously been a fine parish church. Such is the magic of royalty that Leicester now has an assured place in the pantheon of English cathedrals.

L incoln Cathedral was rebuilt in the Gothic style between 1185 and 1311. Then for 248 years it was the tallest building in the world, taller even than the Great Pyramid of Giza, until its spire was blown down in a storm in 1549. It remains an exceptionally large cathedral, in Britain exceeded in floor area only by York Minster and St Paul's Cathedral in London. The Victorian writer John Ruskin wrote: 'I have always held that the cathedral of Lincoln is out and out the most precious piece of architecture in the British Isles and roughly speaking worth any two other cathedrals we have'. It was referred to as the Ark on the Waters since, like Ely Cathedral (see 'Ship of the Fens'), it appears to float above the flat, watery fen landscape that surrounds it.

The early Gothic building of the late twelfth century was largely the work of St Hugh of Lincoln (1140–1200) who, having been born in eastern France, became a Carthusian monk, an order noted for its austerity and observation of strict rules of silence. Henry II, in an act of penance for the murder of Thomas à Becket (see 'Saints and sinners'), had decided to set up a Carthusian house in England instead of going on Crusade, inviting the saintly Hugh to England to help in this enterprise – during a further bout of piety Henry appointed Hugh as Bishop of Lincoln in 1186. However Henry didn't have much luck with his bishops. Hugh excommunicated one of Henry's servants and risked giving further offence by turning down one of the king's candidates for a post at Lincoln. But on this occasion Henry, no doubt wishing to avoid further trouble with the church, controlled his fiery temper and Hugh was forgiven.

Hugh's cathedral was not the first cathedral for the huge diocese of Lincoln, stretching from the Humber to the Thames. The first was in fact the abbey at Dorchester-on-Thames

The Ark on the Waters

in Oxfordshire until a cathedral was built at Lincoln itself, which was completed in 1092. This original structure lasted less than a century, being destroyed by an earthquake on 15 April 1185 that was one of the strongest ever felt in Great Britain, estimated to have registered five on the Richter scale. A later Bishop of Lincoln, Hugh of Wells, was present at the sealing of Magna Carta and the cathedral possesses one of the original copies, briefly loaned to the USA and now securely on display within Lincoln Castle.

EYES AND IMPS
Lincoln Cathedral has two very fine rose windows: in the north transept,

the Dean's Eye that was completed in 1235; and looking towards it in the south transept, the Bishop's Eye that was completed in 1330. A contemporary account entitled **The Metrical Life of St Hugh** *explained that the eyes were on watch for 'the candelabra of Heaven and the darkness of Lethe'. The cathedral is also celebrated for the Lincoln imp, a unique figure in an English cathedral, supposedly a mischievous imp turned to stone while in conversation with a reproving angel at whom the imp was throwing rocks!*

The Lincoln imp

Little Hugh
Cathedral benefits from his cult

Lincoln has not always enjoyed a happy relationship with its Jewish community. The city claims to have the oldest building in England used as a retail outlet, the Jew's House on Steep Hill. This dates from around 1150 and much of the original building survives today, including the frontage onto the street. However in August 1255 the body of a nine-year-old boy named Hugh was found in a well, and for reasons that are obscure the population became convinced that the city's thriving Jewish community had kidnapped, tortured and murdered the child. Anti-Semitic riots followed – not an unusual phenomenon in medieval England – and many Jews were arrested and tortured to extract confessions, while 18 were hanged.

King Henry III encouraged this process – as usual he was short of money, thus decreeing that any property belonging to Jews convicted of a crime would pass to him. Lincoln Cathedral was to benefit from this discreditable episode since the cult of

Little Hugh drew many pilgrims, the event being referred to by Chaucer in his *Prioress's Tale*. The child never officially became St Hugh, although he was informally awarded that title by many who visited his tomb, these pilgrims continuing to arrive as late as the twentieth century. In 1955 the cathedral placed a plaque by the remains of Little Hugh's shrine, asking for forgiveness for the sufferings of Lincoln's Jews.

Henry's son, Edward I, continued this horrible tradition of persecution and confiscation, and in 1290 he simply expelled all the Jews from England, confiscating their property. They had to wait 350 years before they were invited back by Oliver Cromwell. Edward I did confer a benefit on the cathedral when he passed through the city with the body of his much-loved wife, Eleanor of Castile, who had died in 1290 at Harby in Nottinghamshire. Her body was embalmed in Lincoln, during which some of her entrails were removed and buried in Lincoln Cathedral, where Edward placed a replica of the tomb she eventually occupied in Westminster Abbey.

Dam busters
*Home to the brave
bomber squadrons*

In World War II the flat lands surrounding Lincoln Cathedral were home to many bomber stations, among them RAF Scampton where 617 Squadron, the Dam Busters, were based. Lincoln Cathedral features in the film of the same name, as the aircraft take off on their perilous journey to attack the Ruhr dams. The squadron took as its motto a phrase attributed to King Louis XV of France, '*Après moi, le déluge*', which means 'After me the flood', a premonition of the French Revolution that followed his death.

Meanwhile the station badge for nearby RAF Waddington features Lincoln Cathedral rising through the clouds, and it is therefore appropriate that Lincoln is the only cathedral to house a memorial to the 55,000 members of bomber crews who died in the war. The cathedral also houses the tomb of Katherine Swynford – wife of John of Gaunt, Duke of Lancaster, who was the son of Edward III, the brother of the Black Prince, and father to the future King Henry IV. Katherine Swynford's sister, Philippa, married the poet Geoffrey Chaucer.

ALIAS WESTMINSTER
On two occasions Lincoln Cathedral has been used as a substitute for Westminster Abbey. The abbey refused a request to be used for filming The Da Vinci Code, so Lincoln stepped in and for a while accommodated a polystyrene replica of the tomb of Sir Isaac Newton, the original of which is to be found in the abbey. Again it stood in for the abbey in 2007, this time for the filming of The Young Victoria.

LIVERPOOL ANGLICAN CATHEDRAL

Longest and largest
Built by an inexperienced architect

L iverpool's Anglican cathedral, like that of Durham, occupies a particularly spectacular site, built as it is on St James's Mount, one of the highest points in one of Britain's flattest cities. Besides its prominent position it is also the longest cathedral in the world, measuring 189 metres (620 feet) in length, as well as over a hundred metres in height – it also has a claim to being the world's largest Anglican church building in internal space.

In the nineteenth century Liverpool's population expanded rapidly, through trade with America and the influx of Irish immigrants fleeing the potato famine of 1845 to 1852. By 1877 the population was approaching 700,000 and while the Catholics, accounting for about a quarter of the residents, already had a bishop and plans for a cathedral (see 'Paddy's Wigwam'), the Anglican majority had to wait until 1880 for the appointment of its first bishop. At first this new bishop had to make do with a temporary cathedral in the form of the parish church of St Peter's on Church Street, which was neither large enough nor very attractive.

Then in 1902 Parliament approved the construction of a cathedral, only the third Anglican cathedral to be built since the Reformation – the others being Christopher Wren's St Paul's (see 'On top of the world'), which was rebuilt after the fire of 1665, and Truro (see 'Serving Cornwall'). The competition for designing this new cathedral attracted 103 entries, including submissions from eminent architects such as the Scot Charles Rennie Mackintosh (1868–1928), designer of such fine buildings as the Glasgow School of Art.

To the amazement of many, the 22-year-old Giles Gilbert Scott (1880–1960) won the competition. Although the descendant of a famous family (see 'An architectural dynasty'), Scott was still working as a pupil in the practice of another architect who had been a pupil of Scott's father – Scott was also a Catholic. By his own admission, Scott's only design to that point had been one for a pipe rack. So when the Cathedral Committee accepted his design, as a precaution they also appointed the eminent Victorian architect George Bodley (1827–1907) to work with him. The two men did not get on and it was fortunate for Scott (although not for

Bodley) that Bodley died in 1907, just as work was getting under way.

Like Wren, another architect with limited experience (see 'A bold but fortunate choice'), Scott made many alterations to his design as work progressed, so the cathedral he built had one central tower (instead of two at the west end) and two transepts (instead of one). Despite these alterations and the intervention of two world wars, during the second of which Liverpool was particularly

Liverpool Anglican Cathedral

badly bombed, the cathedral was substantially complete by 1961, Scott having died the previous year.

The cathedral was consecrated in October 1978 in the presence of David Sheppard, Bishop of Liverpool and former England cricketer, as well as the Roman Catholic Archbishop Derek Warlock. Besides its interesting history and stunning architecture, the cathedral also has the largest bell tower in the world, the heaviest bells at 16.5 tons, and the largest pipe organ in Great Britain.

LIVERPOOL METROPOLITAN CATHEDRAL

Paddy's Wigwam
Instigated by famine and built by four architects

Liverpool's Catholic Cathedral is unique in owing its existence to a terrible famine. In 1845 potato blight struck the staple food of Irish peasants, causing mass starvation, death and emigration, with many of the victims leaving the country

for England and many more for the USA. The famine helped to ignite the demand for Irish independence from Great Britain, but more immediately it caused an influx of desperate people to ports facing Ireland, notably Glasgow and Liverpool. At the time the population of Ireland fell by a quarter and even now it has not returned to the level seen prior to the famine.

The Catholic Bishop of Liverpool, Alexander Goss (1814–72), saw the need for a cathedral to serve the burgeoning Irish population of the city so he commissioned Edward Welby Pugin (1833–75) to submit a suitable design. Pugin, the son of A. W. N. Pugin who was involved in designing the Palace of Westminster, was the first of four architects to be involved in creating the new cathedral over a period of more than a century. By 1856 he was building the Lady Chapel when the project ran out of money and work was suspended – the Lady Chapel subsequently served as a parish church until it was demolished in the 1980s.

The next architect to try his hand was Sir Edwin Lutyens (1869–1944),

Paddy's Wigwam or the Mersey Funnel

designer of New Delhi, whose cathedral would have been second only to St Peter's Basilica, Rome in size with a dome 20 per cent larger. Work began in 1933 but halted in 1941, owing to the exigencies of World War II. In 1956 work resumed and by 1958 the crypt was completed, whereupon work halted again – a model of the Lutyens design may still be seen at the Museum of Liverpool. At this point the Catholic hierarchy turned to the ever-reliable Scott family for assistance. At the time Sir Giles Gilbert Scott (see 'An architectural dynasty') was at work

on Liverpool's Anglican Cathedral so they asked his younger brother, Adrian, to turn his hand to its Catholic counterpart. He proposed a scaled-down version of the Lutyens edifice – but that too was rejected.

Finally Sir Frederick Gibberd (1908–84) was asked to assist, whose reputation to that point had mostly been made in housing schemes, although he also designed Didcot Power Station and the London Central Mosque in Regent's Park. Gibberd was asked to incorporate Lutyens' crypt into his design and accommodate a congregation of 2,000, which he achieved by designing a circular building with the altar at the centre, visible to all. The cathedral is surmounted by a conical structure with the appearance of a funnel, which in reference to the city's Irish population quickly earned it the name of Paddy's Wigwam or the Mersey Funnel.

This took only five years to build between 1962 and 1967, and is one of the most striking features of the Liverpool skyline, despite competing with the Anglican Cathedral and the Three Graces on the waterfront – the Royal Liver Building, the Cunard Building and the Port of Liverpool Building. No other English city displays such a fine array of buildings from two centuries.

BEER IN THE BASEMENT
Sir Edwin Lutyens' crypt at Liverpool Metropolitan Cathedral serves a number of unusual purposes. Besides accommodating examinations for the University of Liverpool it also, in a more jovial spirit, hosts an annual beer festival that draws visitors from Europe, the USA and Australia. Given the

large Irish element of the Liverpool population, one may feel confident that Guinness is well represented among the drinks on offer.

MANCHESTER CATHEDRAL

Changing fortunes
A cathedral and a diocese for Cottonopolis

Like its neighbour and rival city Liverpool, Manchester developed extremely rapidly in the nineteenth century. From being a small market town at the beginning of the century, by 1850 it had become known as 'Cottonopolis', the centre of the world's trade in cotton, and was surrounded by a network of canals, railways and mill towns that made it the world's leading industrial settlement. In 1854 it was officially made a city by letters patent issued by Queen Victoria, the first new city in Great Britain for three centuries.

The first Bishop of Manchester had been appointed six years earlier in 1848. As his cathedral, he acquired a building that was four centuries old, although a Saxon church had existed on the site since about 700. The later fourteenth-century church was known as the Collegiate Church of St Mary, St Denys and St George, St Denys being chosen because an aristocratic priest named Thomas de la Warre of French descent had founded it. At that time the building served as a church for a college of priests and also as a parish church.

Much of the building dates from the Tudor period of the late fifteenth and early sixteenth century and was undertaken as a result of aristocratic patronage from the most influential circles. James Stanley was a descendant of the Stanley family (later Earls of Derby) whose timely intervention had turned the Battle of Bosworth in favour of Henry Tudor (later Henry VII) in 1485 at the expense of Richard III (see 'King in the car park'). His patronage could therefore afford the best craftsmen and there is evidence that much of the work was carried out by John Wastell, one of the foremost stonemasons of his age and creator

of the later stages of King's College Chapel in Cambridge with its famous fan vault. Other work was paid for by the de Trafford family, whose name is now more often associated with football and cricket than architecture.

The college suffered many changes of fortune during the religious turbulence of the Tudor period, but Elizabeth I eventually restored its fortunes when she appointed as warden the mathematician and astrologer John Dee (1527–1609). Dee has been identified as the model for Prospero in Shakespeare's final play *The Tempest,* and his former lodging now accommodates Chetham's Library – founded in 1653, this is the oldest public library in the English speaking world. The college's church prospered as a parish church, and in 1840 its warden and clergy became dean and canons in preparation for it becoming the cathedral for the new diocese of Manchester. The building was extensively refurbished in 1882 but the finest medieval work survives, notably 14 angels carved into the nave roof, each playing a different musical instrument.

NEWCASTLE CATHEDRAL

Lantern landmark
Cathedral serves ships on the sea

Newcastle's lantern tower

Newcastle's Cathedral Church of St Nicholas serves the most northerly diocese in the Church of England. It was originally built in 1091, during the reign of William the Conqueror's son William Rufus, close to the site of the castle from which the city takes its name and to the earlier site of Hadrian's Wall, now lost amidst the buildings of the later city. The dedication to St Nicholas, the patron saint of sailors and boats, probably owes much to Newcastle's long association with the sea and shipbuilding. Indeed the cathedral's conspicuous lantern tower long served as a landmark for ships navigating the North Sea and the Tyne, a lantern tower being more often associated with churches across the border in Scotland.

The cathedral's lantern tower is decorated with some very unusual Old Testament statues that depict:

Adam eating the apple; Eve proffering it; Aaron, the elder brother of Moses, improbably arrayed as a bishop; and David playing his harp. The lantern tower had a narrow escape after an invasion of the city by Scottish forces in 1644, during the last of the civil wars of the 1640s. Faced with a threat by the Scots to bombard the tower, the Mayor of Newcastle, Sir John Marley, informed the invaders that he was holding his Scottish prisoners there. The cathedral's monuments include one that celebrates Admiral Collingwood (1740–1810) who took command of the British fleet after the death of Nelson at the Battle of Trafalgar.

NORWICH CATHEDRAL

Resolutely Norman
But pillaged by a Puritan mob

Norwich Cathedral, which was mostly built between 1096 and 1145, remains a resolutely Norman building with just the addition of a unique two-storey cloister from

Norwich Cathedral

1297. This latter project could be afforded because at the time Norwich, the third city in England after London and Bristol, was prospering from the medieval wool trade that thrived in East Anglia.

Nowadays the cathedral is second only to Salisbury in the height of its spire, which had to be rebuilt after it was struck by lightning in 1463 with such force that the resulting fire turned the limestone in the nave pink, and the size of its Cathedral Close (see 'A very large Close') – although the Close actually has more occupants than that of Salisbury. Behind the high altar is the only bishop's throne in the UK that still contains fragments of the Saxon original.

The cathedral survived the Tudor reformers better than most, but during the English Civil War (1642–51) it had the misfortune to be located in East Anglia, which was an area overwhelmingly sympathetic to Parliament. In 1643, along with many other East Anglian churches, it was pillaged by a Puritan mob and lay virtually abandoned for 20 years until it was restored, following the return to the throne of Charles II.

'Patriotism is not enough'
A celebrated memorial to Edith Cavell

Edith Cavell

Norwich Cathedral holds the grave of Edith Cavell (1865–1915), a British nurse who was shot by a German firing squad in Belgium on 12 October 1915 for treason after she confessed to aiding the escape of almost 200 Allied soldiers fleeing from the German occupiers. According to the rules of war, as then applied by the Geneva Convention, the Germans were legally justified in executing her, although some prominent German citizens had argued for clemency.

Her execution proved to be a source of powerful propaganda for the Allied cause and her body was returned to Norwich – she had been born in the village of Swardeston to the south of the city where her father was a clergyman. There is also a memorial to her in St Martin's Place, just off Trafalgar Square in London, on which are inscribed the words she uttered to the clergyman who gave her communion the night before her execution: 'Patriotism is not enough. I must have no hatred or bitterness towards anyone.'

A less celebrated association with the cathedral concerns the Reverend Harold Davidson (1875–1937), who attained brief notoriety in the 1930s. A graduate of Oxford, he had an interest in the world of the theatre and a genuine concern for the poor. After being ordained, in 1906 he was appointed Rector of Stiffkey (pronounced 'Stewkey') in Norfolk where he was popular with his parishioners, especially the poorer ones he helped from his own pocket.

Unfortunately he antagonized a local grandee, who was offended by Davidson's habit of making trips to London during the week to meet young women, and according to Davidson, save them from sinful lives. Others thought he had less noble motives, so following a protracted process involving private detectives, faked photographs and a great deal of interest from the popular press, he was summoned to a hearing at Norwich Cathedral. Davidson arrived at the cathedral to loud applause and later emerged unfrocked, or deprived of his priestly office, proclaiming 'I have been known as the prostitutes' Padre, the proudest title that a true priest of Christ can hold'.

Davidson went on to earn a precarious living as a public entertainer before being killed by a lion in a cage at a Skegness amusement park in 1937. His former parishioners, cherishing his memory, requested that he be buried in Stiffkey where they tended his grave with affection and care.

OXFORD CATHEDRAL

Peculiar status
Unique as both a cathedral and chapel

The site of Oxford Cathedral was originally the convent of St Frideswide (c. 650–735), a Mercian princess. She escaped an undesirable suitor by hiding among swine, miraculously creating a well that may still be seen in the grounds of St Margaret's Church at Binsey to the north of Oxford – this well was to become the inspiration for the one of treacle about which Lewis Carroll wrote in *Alice in Wonderland*. Meanwhile St Frideswide went on to become the patron saint of Oxford and its university.

Oxford Cathedral's rather stumpy spire, dating from 1230, is the oldest in England, and the cathedral is unique in being both the cathedral of the diocese of Oxford as well as the chapel of Christ Church, Oxford University's largest college. It owes this peculiar status to Cardinal

Thomas Wolsey (1474–1530), who fell from favour when he failed to arrange Henry VIII's (1491–1547) divorce from Catherine of Aragon. In 1522 Wolsey decided that he wanted the site for his new Cardinal College, which would be equal in magnificence to his palace at Hampton Court. Wolsey was at the height of his power and not a man much troubled by humility, so although this was a full decade before his master the king fell foul of Rome, Wolsey simply helped himself to the church of St Frideswide's convent, demolishing the western end to make room for what was to become Tom Quad, the largest college quadrangle in Oxford.

In 1529, as Henry VIII started to become disillusioned with his Lord Chancellor Wolsey, the king took over the Cardinal College and in 1546 he created the new diocese of Oxford, appointing the college chapel as its cathedral. Off the south transept, St Lucy's Chapel contains a window depicting Thomas à Becket that surprisingly survived the attentions of the Tudor vandals – a quick-thinking priest removed the

Cardinal Thomas Wolsey

face of the archbishop, replacing it with a piece of plain glass. So Becket survived that first onslaught, but without his face. The window would also survive the attentions of the Puritans, despite the fact that for a time during the English Civil War (1642–51) the city was the capital of Charles I who lived at Christ Church – the cathedral therefore contains some Civil War memorials.

To this day the Dean of Oxford Cathedral is also the Dean of Christ

Church, Oxford's largest college. When Henry VIII re-founded the college he renamed it Aedes Christi, which means the House of Christ, thus Christ Church – in Oxford the college is commonly referred to as simply the House. The official title of the foundation is the Dean, Chapter and Students of the Cathedral Church of Christ in Oxford of the Foundation of King Henry the Eighth, so the Fellows or teaching staff of the college are confusingly known as Students. What do they call the undergraduates? The answer is also Students!

I do not like thee Dr Fell,
The reason why I cannot tell;
But this I know, and know
   full well,
I do not like thee, Dr Fell.

The cathedral also holds the grave of Henry Liddell (1811–98), father of Alice Liddell who became the inspiration for Lewis Carroll's **Alice in Wonderland.** *Henry Liddell and Lewis Carroll (1832–98, whose real name was Charles Ludwidge Dodgson) were contemporaries at Christ Church, Liddell being a classical scholar and dean at the college, while Lewis Carroll was a Student of mathematics.*

NOTABLE BURIALS

Oxford Cathedral is host to a number of notable burials. John Locke (1632–1704) the philosopher, who argued for the extension of religious tolerance following the English Civil War and whose ideas of liberty strongly influenced the Constitution of the USA, is buried in the cathedral, as is Dr John Fell (1625–86), Dean of Christ Church and also Bishop of Oxford who, after falling out with an undergraduate named Tom Brown, inspired the verse:

ST PATRICK'S CATHEDRAL, DUBLIN

Protestant establishment
*A matter of dispute
for eight centuries*

It may come as a surprise to many visitors to Ireland's capital that the cathedral named after the saint of what is surely one of the world's most Catholic nations is in fact a Protestant establishment with allegiance to the Church of Ireland. And a further surprise follows, since the city actually has two cathedrals – and the other, Christ Church, is also Protestant. The relative status of the two cathedrals was a matter of dispute for eight centuries, only just about resolved in 1870.

St Patrick, who lived in the fifth century, is the subject of many legends. However it is reasonably certain that he was born in Roman Britain before being kidnapped by pirates and taken to Ireland where, with the status of a slave, he worked as a shepherd and became a follower of

Christ. After six years he fled back to Britain then spent some time studying in France, possibly at Auxerre where he was ordained, before returning to Ireland as a missionary. He is known as the Apostle of Ireland and is said to have baptized people at a well beside Dublin's River Poddle, which still runs beneath Patrick Street before entering the River Liffey – a small wooden church stood on

St Patrick, Ireland's patron saint

the site during Patrick's lifetime.

In 1154, allegedly at the invitation of Pope Adrian IV, Henry II of England decided to involve himself in the affairs of Ireland and a Norman Archbishop of Dublin was appointed without consulting the Irish. This archbishop decided to elevate the small church dedicated to St Patrick – which had replaced the original one the saint knew – to the status of a cathedral. The precise date that St Patrick's became a cathedral is not certain, but since a dean took office in 1219, it must have been a cathedral by that date. This was despite the fact that Dublin already had a cathedral, Christ Church, which served the diocese of Dublin.

The reason for creating a second cathedral in a small city is far from clear yet it ensured that relations between the two were tense until 1300, when a peace treaty of sorts was agreed. This acknowledged that: both buildings were cathedrals; the enthronement of the Archbishop of Dublin would take place at Christ Church, a practice not always followed; Christ Church was to have formal precedence; and deceased archbishops would be buried alternately in the two cathedrals.

This arrangement continued, more or less to the satisfaction of both parties, until 1870, when St Patrick's was designated as the cathedral for the whole of Ireland – rather like Canterbury for England – while Christ Church became the seat for the Archbishop of Dublin. St Patrick's is the larger building – in fact it is the largest church in Ireland – but it has no crypt, owing to the high water table created by the proximity of the River Poddle where St Patrick had performed his baptisms.

TWO FUNERALS

Despite the Anglican status of St Patrick's, many Irish state occasions have taken place in this Protestant cathedral. The funeral of two Irish Presidents were held there: Douglas Hyde in 1949 then Erskine Childers in 1974. At Hyde's funeral the Irish government and opposition remained in the foyer while the funeral took place – in 1949 Catholics were forbidden by the Pope to attend services in churches that it regarded as Protestant. By

1974 rules had relaxed a little and the funeral of Erskine Childers was attended by Irish statesmen, as well as by Earl Mountbatten on behalf of Elizabeth II, and the British Prime Minister, Harold Wilson.

Enter the Reformation
Things become even more complicated

To make things a little more complicated, during the reign of Henry VIII, when the king broke from the Roman Catholic Church, St Patrick's Cathedral became an Anglican Church of Ireland cathedral before being demoted, by the more severely Protestant Edward VI, to the status of parish church. This left Christ Church as the only cathedral and a thoroughly Protestant one at that. Mary I restored St Patrick's status – along with the silverware and other treasures that had been transferred to Christ Church – but Elizabeth I made St Patrick's a Protestant cathedral again. This meant that once more Dublin had two cathedrals, both Anglican and both situated in an area where, although within the Pale, the majority of inhabitants were Catholics.

However St Patrick's troubles were not over. Oliver Cromwell, who regarded the Anglican Church as a little too Catholic for his liking, stabled his horses there while dealing with his Irish insurgents. After his death the cathedral's life resumed a more tranquil course and in 1666 it offered the use of its Lady Chapel to Huguenots, the French Protestants fleeing the persecution of Louis XIV. This use continued, with services in French, until 1816, by which time all the Huguenots' descendants were attending services in English.

And to make things a little more complicated still, the Catholic Archbishop of Dublin still lays formal claim to Christ Church as his cathedral but uses nearby St Mary's Church as his pro-cathedral, or acting cathedral, while Christ Church continues to be used as by the Anglican archbishop as his cathedral. But these two archbishops seem to get on pretty well.

BEYOND THE PALE

When the Plantagenet kings, beginning with Henry II, invaded Ireland, at first they settled much of the country. However as the incomers were absorbed into the local population, often inter-marrying, the area directly administered by the crown diminished until it extended for only a few dozen miles around Dublin. This area became known as the Pale, derived from the Latin word **palus** *that means a stake or fence, and in places such as Clane in County Kildare parts of this boundary fence may still be seen. Today the expression is used in Ireland to refer to Dublin and its surrounding area. Most of the British families who administered Ireland before the country's independence lived within the Pale but the great majority of the inhabitants were still Catholic Irish, served by its two Protestant cathedrals.*

Disappointed expectations

Two deans – a gambler and a bitter satirist

The most celebrated of all the deans of St Patrick's is undoubtedly Jonathan Swift. But first we must mention Dean Pakenham (1843–64), who was responsible for much of the restoration work undertaken in the nineteenth century. During the process he discovered a Celtic cross, now preserved in the cathedral, which was thought to come from St Patrick's well. However Pakenham blotted his copybook when he sold some of the cathedral's fireplaces to pay off his gambling debts.

Jonathan Swift (1667–1745) was

Jonathan Swift

related to the poet John Dryden and by marriage to Sir Walter Raleigh, yet his life appears to have been a series of disappointed expectations. His writings reflect his frustrations: he was dissatisfied with the Whig governments of Sir Robert Walpole; and he had close but apparently unconsummated relationships first with Esther Johnson, known as 'Stella', and later with Esther Vanhomrigh. Children often read his famous novel *Gulliver's Travels,* but like much of Swift's work, this is actually a sharp satire on the politics of the day.

Having been ordained after his failure to obtain a diplomatic post, he became Dean of St Patrick's in 1713, holding the position until his death. He wrote his own epitaph, which stands near his burial site in St Patrick's Cathedral and reflects his rather bitter view of life. The epitaph is in Latin – the English translation is as follows:

Here is laid the Body
of Jonathan Swift,
  Doctor of Sacred Theology,
Dean of this Cathedral Church,
where fierce Indignation

can no longer
injure the Heart.
Go forth, Voyager,
and copy, if you can,
this vigorous (to the best of
  his ability)
Champion of Liberty.

HANDEL'S MESSIAH

Handel's **Messiah** *received its first performance in Dublin in 1742, during Jonathan Swift's tenure as Dean of St Patrick's. The performance was held in the Great Music Hall in Fishamble Street but the choir for the premiere of Handel's most celebrated work consisted of the choirs of both St Patrick's and Christ Church.*

ST PAUL'S CATHEDRAL

On top of the world
An icon of the City of London

The present St Paul's Cathedral is most likely the fourth version of the cathedral that London has seen – there was possibly one on

Tower Hill whose remains were excavated in 1999, but subsequent cathedrals have all been situated at the top of Ludgate Hill, the highest point within the Square Mile of the City of London itself. Until 1962 St Paul's was the highest and by far the most prominent building in the City, its magnificent dome surrounded by the spires of other City churches, also designed by Sir Christopher Wren to contrast with the dome. Since 1962 many office buildings have sprung up, some outstanding and some hideous, with which St Paul's now has to share the skyline.

There was a cathedral on Ludgate Hill in 962 where Ethelred the Unready was buried, but according to the *Anglo-Saxon Chronicle*, a fire destroyed this in 1087 along with much else in the City. The Norman cathedral, whose construction began in 1087 immediately after the fire, was the first of which records still exist and is commonly referred to as Old St Paul's. Building of the Norman cathedral continued for over two centuries and was not completed until 1314, by which time St Paul's was the longest cathedral in Europe, and with

its medieval spire the tallest, apart from Lincoln whose spire collapsed in 1549 (see 'Taller than the Great Pyramid'). This event left St Paul's as the tallest building in England – and the largest cathedral north of the Alps – until it burned down in the Great Fire of London in 1665, the fire in the building no doubt helped by the fact that the vault of the nave was built of wood rather than stone.

The medieval cathedral had been surrounded by a kind of ecclesiastical village of churches, chapels, shrines and similar buildings. However these were seized by the agents of Henry VIII after the break with Rome and sold as shops and printing works. The centre of London's printing and publishing business remained in Amen Court and Paternoster Row until World War II when bombing set the area ablaze, destroying huge quantities of books. The area's successor, Paternoster Square, is now home to the London Stock Exchange.

St Paul's Cathedral has had a fine choir from its earliest days, consisting of boys with unbroken voices and men who are professional musicians known as Vicars Choral

– the wonderful music in St Paul's inspired Thomas Bisse to instigate the Three Choirs Festival (see 'A fortuitous and friendly proposal'). By the late Tudor period the building was in a poor condition so it was suggested in some quarters that it should be pulled down and replaced by a Classical building like that of St Peter's Basilica in Rome, which was being built although it was not completed until 1606.

UNINTENDED CONSEQUENCES

Some of the money used to build Rome's great cathedral of St Peter's Basilica was raised by the sale of indulgences, grants of forgiveness for sins that didn't ask too many questions about repentance or intentions for future conduct. One of the most zealous agents at raising money for the rebuild in this way was the Archbishop of Mainz, whose behaviour in this so offended German theologian Martin Luther (1483–1546) that he published his **Ninety-Five Theses** *in protest, posting this disputation on the door of All Saints Church in Wittenberg in 1517.*

This act prompted the debates that led to the Protestant Reformation, of which Henry VIII was at first such a vociferous opponent that he published a refutation of Luther's arguments. So impressed was the Pope by the king's zeal that he declared him to be **Fidei Defensor,** *or a Defender of the Faith. How His Holiness must have regretted this act when Henry finally broke with Rome over his divorce. To this day the British monarch promises to defend the faith in the coronation ceremony and the abbreviated words* **Fid Def** *appear on British coins.*

A bold but fortunate choice
With a good knowledge of astronomy and a head for heights

The poor condition of the Norman St Paul's Cathedral prompted calls for its rebuild in the Classical style. As a compromise, a Classical façade was built at the west end of the medieval Gothic cathedral by the architect Inigo Jones but this unusual combination of styles, perhaps fortunately, did not last long – in 1665 the entire building was destroyed in the Great Fire of London.

The task of designing a new cathedral was finally assigned to an Oxford Professor of Astronomy, a man who had a good knowledge of mathematics and was, along with Sir Isaac Newton, a founder of the Royal Society in 1660 – now regarded as the most distinguished and oldest society in the world dedicated to the advancement of science. But despite this promising pedigree this man had little experience in architecture, a discipline for which astronomy is not normally regarded as an appropriate preparation. He had written some theoretical works on the subject but his commissions to that date were limited.

As a favour to his nephew, the eventual architect's uncle, Matthew Wren, Bishop of Ely, had given him the task of building a new chapel for his former college at Cambridge, Pembroke College, whose medieval chapel a Puritan named William Dowsing had desecrated in 1643. The small college chapel was consecrated in 1665 and within three years, in July 1668, its architect, the astronomer Christopher Wren (1632–1723), was given the task by William Sancroft, the Dean of St Paul's, of designing a cathedral that was 'handsome and noble to all the ends of it and to the reputation of the City and the Nation'.

As it turned out the dean had made a bold but fortunate choice. Wren devoted much of the rest of his life to building the cathedral – as well as 51 other City churches – for which he received a stipend of £200 a year, £60 of which he returned to the building fund. His duties included being hauled daily in a basket to the top of the scaffolding to inspect the work.

Royal approval
With permission to make ornamental changes

Appointed as architect to design and rebuild a new St Paul's Cathedral (see 'A bold but fortunate choice'), Christopher Wren needed to please a lot of people – the king, the clergy, the City fathers and advocates of differing architectural styles. One party wanted the old cathedral to be rebuilt from its smouldering ruins, while others advocated a fresh Classical design. It is perhaps not surprising that Wren produced five designs before one was finally chosen that more or less satisfied all parties.

A model illustrated one of the early designs that measures 6 metres (20 feet) in length and 4 metres (13 feet) in height – it is still on show in the cathedral to this day. At the time this attracted so much critical comment that Wren vowed never again to expose his plans to public scrutiny and thereby 'lose time and subject his business many times to incompetent judges' – many architects have no doubt felt such frustrations since his time.

One of Wren's designs had a narrow dome surmounted by a tall spire. This attracted royal approval and was authorized by a royal warrant, although Wren received permission from Charles II to make 'ornamental changes' to the design as he built, a licence he exercised ruthlessly. During the process the spire disappeared and the dome became broader and higher.

In fact, the cathedral's dome comprises three separate structures.

The first is an inner dome seen from within the cathedral. Within this inner dome is the Whispering Gallery, so called because of its strange acoustics, which are such that a whisper against the wall at any point can be heard at any other – the gallery is reached by climbing 260 steps from the floor of the cathedral. Beyond the inner dome is a cone of brick that is invisible but structurally essential. Then there is the outer dome, visible from the exterior, which is familiar to the world and crowned with a cross.

The cathedral was consecrated in 1697, less than 30 years after Wren had received the commission from the dean and despite the delays caused by disputes over the design. The topping out ceremony, when the final stone was placed on the top of the dome, occurred in October 1708. This was executed by Wren's son, also named Christopher, along with the son of one of the cathedral's masons.

SAVE THE CATHEDRAL!
The dome of St Paul's Cathedral was made world famous on 29 December 1940, during the London Blitz, when a photographer named

St Paul's Cathedral

Herbert Mason took a photograph of it, wreathed in smoke and surrounded by fires, from the roof of the **Daily Mail** building off Fleet Street. At the height of the raid Winston Churchill telephoned the London Guildhall – itself destroyed in the Blitz – to tell the authorities that all available fire-fighting equipment should be directed to save the cathedral, thus avoiding further damage to the nation's morale.

In the event three bombs hit the cathedral – two caused damage and one huge bomb failed to explode, which was later defused by Lieutenant Robert Davies and Sapper George Wylie of the Royal Engineers. When this bomb was eventually detonated in a safe location, its explosion formed a crater that measured 30 metres (98 feet) wide. If it had exploded where it had dropped it would most definitely have destroyed the cathedral – both men were subsequently awarded the George Cross.

An unhappy experience
The story of the Gloomy Dean

W illiam Inge (1860–1954) was a most unlikely person to become the dean of a cathedral such as St Paul's that had such a strong musical tradition. A prolific journalist for popular newspapers such as the *Sunday Express* and *Evening Standard*, he used his columns to be highly critical of almost everything, including the Catholic and Anglican Churches for pandering to the working classes. And he regarded the non-availability of servants as a major cause of domestic strife.

Inge became friendly with Charles Darwin's cousin, Francis Galton, and like Galton, he became an advocate of eugenics, which maintained that inferior classes should be discouraged from breeding and if necessary sterilized. He complained that by educating the children of working people and encouraging them to take up professional posts, the government would place the children of the upper classes at a disadvantage in competition with the lower orders.

Inge subsequently made huge sums of money through his lecture tours of the USA and great distress was caused to the clergy of St Paul's when in 1911 Prime Minister Asquith offered Inge the post of dean. This did not turn out to be a happy experience, not least because the new dean didn't like music. When Queen Mary commented on what a privilege it was for him to hear such wonderful services, he assured the queen that, far from enjoying it, he found it irksome and doubted whether God appreciated it either. He thus became known as the Gloomy Dean, living to the age of 94.

Potential disfigurement
The dispute over Wellington's horse

S t Paul's Cathedral rivals Westminster Abbey for the number of tombs and memorials it accommodates of the great and the good. The largest monument belongs to Arthur Wellesley, 1st Duke of Wellington (1769–1852), who was awarded the rare honour for a person not of royal blood of a state funeral. Huge crowds attended his funeral procession on 18 November 1852 when the Iron Duke's body was taken to St Paul's.

The funeral was followed by a dispute about whether his monument should support a statue of Wellington seated upon his horse Copenhagen, on the grounds that a horse would disfigure the abbey – after 60 years in 1912 the statue was added. A similar statue may be seen outside the Bank of England with one serious omission – the sculptor forgot to add the stirrups.

Wellington's tomb is in the crypt next to that of Admiral Horatio Nelson (1758–1805). After his death at the Battle of Trafalgar, Nelson's body was brought to England in a barrel of brandy to preserve it then laid in a coffin made from the timbers of the French warship *L'Orient,* which he had destroyed at the Battle of the Nile. The coffin was placed in a marble sarcophagus designed for Cardinal Wolsey that was found lying around at Windsor, unused after the cardinal's death in 1530, by which time he had fallen out with Henry VIII.

Appropriately the first burial and

Duke of Wellington's statue

the most intriguing monument to be found is one to the cathedral's architect, Sir Christopher Wren. His tomb is a simple stone slab above which a stone panel is inscribed with the words '*Lector, Si Monumentum Requiris, Circumspice*'. This translates as 'Reader, if you require his monument, look around you'.

Among many other memorials are those to Florence Nightingale, Sir

Alexander Fleming, J. M. W. Turner, Lawrence of Arabia and the composer of *Jerusalem,* Sir Hubert Parry. The oldest monument in the cathedral, and the only one to survive the Great Fire of London intact, is that of the dean and poet John Donne. He posed for the monument before his death and is depicted wrapped in a burial shroud, standing on a funeral urn.

JOHN DONNE, DEAN OF ST PAUL'S

John Donne (1572–1631) is probably the best known of the deans of St Paul's Cathedral. He was the son of Catholic parents in the late sixteenth century, when to be a Catholic was to be regarded as a traitor. His father died when he was four, while his mother was a great-niece of Sir Thomas More who had been executed for treason under Henry VIII – hardly a promising start in life.

He attended both Oxford and Cambridge universities, but as a Catholic he was unable to take a degree. He therefore scraped a modest living as a lawyer and married Anne More, contrary to the wishes of both their families, which earned him a spell in prison and ended his hopes of entering into a career as a diplomat. In 1615 he took holy orders to become an Anglican priest but in 1617 his wife died after giving birth to their twelfth child.

In 1621 he was appointed to the lucrative position of Dean of St Paul's, and following a severe illness, he wrote a series of meditations, which included two of the phrases (often misquoted) for which he is best remembered: 'Never send to know for whom the bell tolls; it tolls for thee', and 'No man is an island entire of itself'. Now he is regarded as one of the greatest love poets of all time

For whom the bell tolls
Meet Great Paul and Great Tom

St Paul's Cathedral contains a full complement of bells, mostly manufactured in the 1870s by the company Taylor of Loughborough. It also has one of the largest bells ever made: Great Paul, cast in 1881 and sounding at one o'clock each day, weighs 16½ tons and was the largest bell in the British Isles until the

Olympic Bell was cast for the 2012
London Olympic Games. Meanwhile
Great Tom tolls to mark the death
of a member of the royal family and
was last heard marking the death of
Queen Elizabeth, the Queen Mother
in 2002. The south-west tower of
the cathedral has a clock designed
by Lord Grimthorpe who designed
the Big Ben mechanism – St Paul's
does not appear to have had as much
trouble accommodating Grimthorpe's
whims as the unfortunate architect
of the Parliamentary clock (see 'Force
of nature').

PETERBOROUGH CATHEDRAL

An ill-treated queen
The grave of Catherine of Aragon

Catherine of Aragon, a wronged queen

Peterborough Cathedral traces
its roots back to 655 but the
Hedda Stone, still held in the Lady
Chapel, commemorates the sacking
of the original building by Vikings in
864. The troubles did not end there.
The disturbances associated with
the rebellion of Hereward the Wake
following the Norman Conquest
led to further destruction and it was
not until 1118 that construction
of the present Norman building
started as an abbey church. This was
dedicated, like its predecessors, to
St Peter and soon gave its name to
the surrounding borough, which
thus became Peterborough.

The nave has a ceiling that is

unique in Britain – a long, painted, wooden ceiling constructed between 1230 and 1250, which now much restored, remains a distinctive feature of the building. The abbey was built of limestone taken from the quarries at Barnack, which the abbey had acquired and was to prove a very shrewd investment – the stone was later used to build Ramsey Abbey, Ely Cathedral and several Cambridge Colleges at great profit to the abbey.

Barnack stone was not the abbey's only asset during the Middle Ages. It also claimed to possess a piece of Aaron's rod, and the remains of the five loaves that fed the 5,000 according to the Gospel of St Luke – abbeys used relics like these to attract pilgrims. However these relics were lost when Henry VIII dissolved the abbey and its church became a cathedral for the diocese of Peterborough.

Yet Henry VIII inadvertently supplied the newly created cathedral with a monument that proved very attractive to visitors. After her divorce his ill-used first wife, Catherine of Aragon (1485–1536), lived at Kimbolton Castle, south of Peterborough. She was buried in Peterborough Cathedral where her grave attracted many visitors, as it still does. Her symbol was the pomegranate, ironically also one of fertility – Henry divorced her because she could not bear him a healthy son. Anne Boleyn, her successor as queen, miscarried a son on the day of Catherine's funeral – a son who, if born healthy, would probably have saved Anne from execution.

Another unfortunate queen later temporarily joined Catherine when the body of Mary, Queen of Scots, was buried at Peterborough, following her execution at nearby Fotheringay in 1587. In 1612 her remains were moved to Westminster Abbey on the orders of her son, James I.

ROCHESTER CATHEDRAL

'Greatly disappointed'
Unwelcome visitors leave the cathedral in a poor condition

Rochester Cathedral, although originally founded by Justus

Anne of Cleves

owner who misappropriated the cathedral's revenues and left its clergy living in extremely poor conditions.

The Archbishop of Canterbury eventually dismissed Odo then appointed another Norman named Gundulf as bishop, who began to construct a new cathedral. He started by building a tower that is named after him, Gundulf's Tower, the lower part of which still remains. But the cathedral's misfortunes at the hands of unwelcome visitors were not over. In 1215, during the wars that marked the final stages of King John's disastrous reign, the cathedral was looted during the siege of Rochester Castle and in 1264, when the city was yet again under siege, it was desecrated by the forces of Simon de Montfort.

Rochester's bishops did not fare well under the Tudors. In 1504 John Fisher was appointed as bishop, a post that he held for the rest of his life. Having been tutor to the young Prince Henry, Fisher remained his strong supporter until the 'King's Great Matter', Henry VIII's divorce from Catherine of Aragon, divided them when the bishop held steadfast for Rome. For

who accompanied St Augustine to nearby Canterbury in 597, has been singularly unfortunate in its visitors. Having been ravaged by the King of Mercia in 676 and borne the brunt of Viking raids, the cathedral's fortunes appeared to change when William the Conqueror passed it to his half-brother Odo, Bishop of Bayeux. However despite his episcopal status Bishop Odo proved a very neglectful this Fisher, by then a cardinal, was beheaded in 1535, becoming a saint in 1935. In 1547 Nicholas Ridley became bishop during the reign of the Protestant Edward VI – but in the following reign of Catholic Mary I he was burned at the stake in Oxford for treason and heresy.

Meanwhile on 1 January 1540 Henry VIII met his fourth wife, Anne of Cleves, at Rochester and was 'greatly disappointed'. The marriage was a brief one that led to the death of Thomas Cromwell in 1540, the scourge of the monasteries who had suggested the match. After Henry VIII's reign the cathedral suffered a decline and in the seventeenth century Archbishop Laud complained about its poor condition, particularly the 'want of glass in the windows'. Worse was to follow in the English Civil War (1642–51) when soldiers from the Parliamentary army entered the cathedral, searching for superstitious objects. Having smashed up some of the furniture, they then 'plucked down the rails and left them for the poor to kindle their fires; and so left the organ to be plucked down when we came back again'.

Twenty years later Samuel Pepys (1633–1703), in his diary, described the cathedral as a 'shabby place'. Hardly surprising, considering the visitors it had had! But on a later visit the great diarist recorded that it was 'fitting for use and the organ then attuning'. Later centuries treated the cathedral more kindly. The fabric was repaired, the furniture replaced, the windows re-glazed, and although Gundulf's Tower was truncated, the lower part was repaired and newly roofed, the work being paid for by freemasons and largely carried out by Sir George Gilbert Scott (see 'An architectural dynasty').

DYING WISH DENIED

Dickens lived for much of his life at Gad's Hill Place just outside Rochester, dying there in 1870. He expressed a wish to be buried in the churchyard of Rochester Cathedral, but as with his contemporary and fellow resident of Kent, Charles Darwin, the nation decided otherwise. Dickens was buried in Westminster Abbey, occupying a part of Poets' Corner (see 'Stone of Destiny').

SALISBURY CATHEDRAL

Rotten borough
*Old Sarum, a constituency
with no voters*

The Cathedral Church of the Blessed Virgin Mary at Salisbury dates from the early thirteenth century, although its origins and those of its bishopric are much earlier. The original settlement in the area lay 3 kilometres (2 miles) to the north of the present city where there are still traces of an Iron Age hill fort, a later Roman garrison and a fortified Saxon settlement called Scarisbyrig, which was later shortened to Sarum or Old Sarum. The outlines of this abandoned site, with fortifications and a church, are clearly visible from a nearby hill, and for many years after the population moved to the city we now know

Old Sarum, a rotten borough

as Salisbury, the word 'Sarum' was used to refer to the new city too.

Old Sarum was gradually deserted but continued to have two Members of Parliament until 1832. Constituencies like Old Sarum became known as rotten boroughs, their MPs, in effect, being nominated by the Lord of the Manor. Old Sarum was not alone in this – Dunwich in Suffolk also continued to have two Members of Parliament into the nineteenth century, despite having been buried beneath the sea by coastal erosion. In 1831 the Great Reform Act abolished Old Sarum, Dunwich and many other rotten boroughs, assigning their Members of Parliament to new cities such as Liverpool and Manchester that had previoulsy been unrepresented.

SARUM USE

The name of Sarum was also preserved in the elaborate Sarum Use, a system of rules for divine service, including the use of different vestments for certain festivals, which originated in the diocese of Salisbury after the Norman conquest. These gradually became more widely adopted, becoming prevalent in English worship until Tudor times then revived during the Oxford Movement of the nineteenth century, when Anglican practices moved closer to those of the Roman Catholic Church.

Celebrated spire
Topping a cathedral built in record time

The Normans created the diocese of Salisbury in 1075 when they abolished the dioceses of Sherborne and Ramsbury near Marlborough, replacing them with the diocese and Bishop of Salisbury. The bishopric remained in Old Sarum until Bishop Richard Poore, who belied his name as a man of great wealth, donated the land on which the new city and cathedral were to be built, close to the River Avon in Wiltshire. The foundation stone for the new cathedral at this new city site was subsequently laid on 28 April 1220.

Salisbury Cathedral was built with almost extraordinary speed by Elias of Dereham (see 'Magna Carta'). Using trees donated by King Henry III and Purbeck limestone from nearby

Teffont Evias, the nave, the transepts and the choir were completed by 1258, all in the Early English style with a fine collection of narrow lancet windows. The cloisters and chapter house followed although the tower, surmounted by a spire, which at 122 metres (404 feet) tall is now the highest in England (but did not always lay claim to this accolade – see 'Taller than the Great Pyramid' and 'On top of the world'), had to wait until 1320.

This aforesaid spire went on to cause great anxiety in the centuries that followed and has been reinforced through the use of buttresses, irons and pillars by architects as eminent as Sir Christopher Wren (see 'On top of the world'). Yet it remains one of the great glories of British architecture, visible from many miles around Salisbury and is memorably celebrated in one of the greatest paintings of John Constable, *Salisbury Cathedral from the Meadows*, which he painted in 1831. The painting had been commissioned by the then Bishop of

Salisbury Cathedral

Salisbury, John Fisher, who is shown in the bottom left-hand corner of the canvas in the company of his wife.

NO BELLS BUT A SIGNIFICANT CHIMING CLOCK

Salisbury Cathedral is one of only three cathedrals that has no bells, the others being Ely and Norwich. The cathedral originally had a fine peal of ten bells, which was housed in a separate bell tower that dated from 1265, but this was occupied by a Parliamentary army during the English Civil War, attacked by Royalist forces and severely damaged. However the cathedral does have a chiming clock dating from 1386, making it the oldest working mechanical clock in the world. This was probably made by three Dutch clockmakers who were invited to England by Edward III and was originally located in the bell tower. When this was demolished in 1792 the clock was temporarily located beneath the spire until it was finally restored and placed on display in the main body of the cathedral, where it continues to chime the hours.

Magna Carta
Home for one of four remaining copies

One of Salisbury Cathedral's greatest treasures is the best one of four surviving original copies of Magna Carta, sealed by a reluctant King John at Runnymede in 1215. Now seen as a seminal document of English constitutional practice, some of its clauses still form parts of the laws of the UK, the USA and many other nations. Salisbury owes its copy

Magna Carta

to the astuteness of one of its builders, Elias of Dereham, who was present at Runnymede and among those entrusted with distributing copies to cathedrals throughout the kingdom.

There is another connection with Magna Carta in the cathedral – the tomb of William Longespee, 3rd Earl of Salisbury (1176–1226). An illegitimate son of Henry II, William was one of the few nobles who remained loyal to his half-brother King John, supporting him in his dispute with the barons at Runnymede. The other tomb of note in the cathedral is that of former Prime Minister Edward Heath (1916–2005), who lived in a house named Arundells in the Cathedral Close for many years and whose memorial service was held at the cathedral.

A very large Close
With a football pitch and literary ties

The Cathedral Close of Salisbury Cathedral is the largest in England, measuring 80 acres in extent. Besides many fine buildings like Arundells, the Queen Anne Mompesson House and two museums, it is also unique in accommodating a football pitch, which is for the use of the boys of the Cathedral School that was founded in Salisbury in 1091 by St Osmund.

In the fourteenth century the cathedral appointed its own constables to safeguard the Close and to collect taxes from its residents. The Close Constabulary survived in one form or another until 2010 when the remaining five constables were disbanded and responsibility was handed over to the Wiltshire Constabulary.

In addition the Close has literary claims to fame. In his autobiography of 1883 Anthony Trollope recorded that while he was 'wandering one evening round the purlieus of Salisbury Cathedral' he 'conceived the story of *The Warden* from which came the series of novels of which Barchester was the central site'. Then Thomas Hardy refers to Salisbury as Melchester is his novels of Wessex.

Later writers have also featured the cathedral in their work. Ken Follett used it as a model for Kingsbridge Cathedral in his novel *The Pillars of* the Earth, and William Golding's novel *The Spire* is a fictional account of Dean Jocelin, whose life is devoted to the building of the magnificent cathedral spire. Golding, who is better known for his novel *The Lord of the Flies,* won the Nobel Prize for literature in 1983, having previously worked as a teacher at Bishop Wordsworth's School in Salisbury.

ON SECOND THOUGHTS, CURRY WILL DO

Of all patron saints St George, the patron saint of England, is surely the most neglected. Yet Salisbury is one of the few English cities where St George's Day is annually celebrated, in the form of a St George's Day Festival of English food. When a British citizen of Bengali descent applied to set up a stall serving curry at the festival her application was rejected on the grounds that curry was not sufficiently English. Since St George himself was Turkish but was later adopted by the English as our patron saint, it seemed only appropriate to some Salisbury citizens that curry, adopted as one of our nation's favourite foods, should

feature in the festival. The organizers of the festival apologized and invited the enterprising lady to participate.

SOUTHWARK CATHEDRAL

A prominent feature
Serving a disreputable area

Southwark Cathedral was a prominent feature of the skyline of the south bank of the River Thames for centuries before it became a cathedral. Thus for five centuries, from 1106 to 1538, it was the church of an Augustinian priory and as such formed part of the huge diocese of Winchester, which at that time extended to the Thames. However an early tradition, reported by historian of London John Stow, was that an earlier priory had been founded by St Swithun during his time as Bishop of Winchester (see 'A bishop's displeasure'). This explains why Swithun is still claimed as founder on an information panel within the cathedral.

The cathedral sits adjacent to

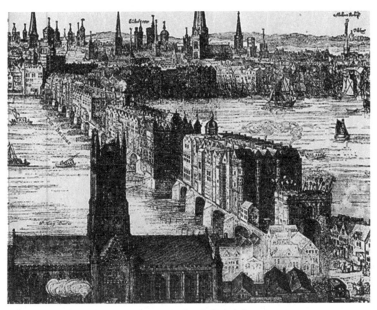

Old London Bridge with St Saviour's, now Southwark Cathedral

Borough Market – trading on its present site since 1014, this is London's oldest market. By the time the Domesday Book was completed around 70 years later in 1086, the Minster of Southwark was under the control of William I's half brother, Bishop Odo of Bayeux, from whom it passed in the reign of Henry I to the Bishop of Winchester. In 1212 the church was destroyed by a fire that reached London Bridge, burning the wooden houses on the bridge but not the bridge itself, which in 1176 had fortunately been rebuilt in stone and thus survived until 1820.

The church was rebuilt, the process beginning in 1220 and continuing for two centuries, to become London's first Gothic church. It served the disreputable entertainment area of the South Bank, where theatres such as the Globe, the Curtain and the Rose were located since they were not permitted within the respectable walls of the City itself across the river – the area also accommodated bear-baiting and cock-fighting arenas. In 1538, when the Augustinian priory was dissolved, it became a parish church named St Saviour's and remained so until 1905 when it became the cathedral for the new diocese of Southwark.

SURVEY OF LONDON

John Stow (c. 1525–1605) was born in Cornhill at the heart of the City of London and devoted his life to collecting written and verbal accounts of the history of the City. To him we owe much of what we know about London in Tudor times and earlier centuries, particularly through his **Survey of London.** *Published in 1598, this survey provides an account of many customs and regulations that governed the City. Stow heard the story of the origins of St Saviour's from the last prior of the Augustinian house before it was suppressed by Henry VIII.*

Lancelot Andrewes, Bishop of Winchester

Theatres and theologians
And two Cambridge connections

Southwark Cathedral contains a number of notable memorials. Edmund Shakespeare (1580–1607), younger brother of the playwright and himself an actor, was buried there and is commemorated by a paving stone. Theatrical entrepreneur, contemporary and patron of Shakespeare, Philip Henslowe

(1560–1616) is also buried in the cathedral, perhaps best remembered through actor Geoffrey Rush's portrayal of Henslowe's character in the film *Shakespeare in Love*. And a stained glass window depicting scenes from Shakespeare's plays celebrates the theatrical traditions of the area.

Meanwhile Lancelot Andrewes, Bishop of Winchester, Master of Pembroke College, Cambridge and one of the principal translators of the King James Bible (also known as the Authorized Version) is buried in a fine tomb within the cathedral. John Harvard, the English minister who emigrated to New England, was baptized there in 1607 and the cathedral has a chapel in his honour, funded by alumni of Harvard University in Cambridge, Massachusetts. Finally the Nelson Mandela monument commemorates the occasion when the statesman opened a new cathedral cloister in 2001.

BISHOP MERVYN STOCKWOOD
One of the most prominent bishops of the Church of England of the
later twentieth century was Mervyn Stockwood, Bishop of Southwark from 1959 to 1980. An avowed socialist and Labour councillor at a time when not many bishops were, he was also a fine preacher, a strong advocate of the needs of the poor who were numerous in his diocese, and an early campaigner for homosexual law reform, although he was himself celibate.

SOUTHWELL MINSTER

The King's Head
Last night of freedom for Charles I

The word 'minster' derives from the Old English *mynster*, meaning a place where the clergy lived and studied together – as in a monastery, which has a similar origin. The word also came to mean 'mother church', from which clergy travelled out in order to minister to congregations who had no resident clergy. From around the year 1000 onwards there developed a system of parishes

Charles I

surviving in the north transept, and was used as a place of worship for the Archbishop of York whose palace stood next to it. The palace is now a ruin but the minster survived, becoming a cathedral in 1884 when the new diocese of Nottingham was created – but it is still referred to as Southwell Minster. During the English Civil War (1642–51), Charles I spent his last night of freedom at an Inn called the King's Head, now the Saracen's Head, in Southwell before surrendering to a Parliamentary army. The troops used the minster as a stable for their horses and ransacked the palace, thus starting the process of its destruction.

LECTERN FROM THE DEPTHS

In 1805 Southwell Minster was given a medieval lectern from Newstead Abbey – at the time home to the poet Lord Byron (1788–1824) – that had survived the Tudor reformers, as the monks had thrown it into a pond to avoid complete destruction. It appears that Lord Byron, not a man noted for his religious observations, does not seem to have missed this lectern.

with their own resident clergy. This meant that minsters became less important, although many kept their names – for example Westminster, Upminster and Southwell Minster.

Southwell Minster dates from Saxon times, with some Saxon work

TEWKESBURY ABBEY

Water and blood
Far, far too much of both

W hen it appears in the news today, Tewkesbury Abbey is most commonly viewed from the air surrounded by water. This is because the town of Tewkesbury lies at the junction of two major rivers, the Severn and the Warwickshire Avon, and is thus exceptionally vulnerable to flooding at times

of heavy rainfall. Fortunately the abbey, one of the world's finest Norman buildings, sits on a hill a short distance from the rivers, thus escaping the worst effects of the floods as it looks down upon its less fortunate neighbours. However the abbey has witnessed one of the most bloody episodes in English history.

We owe the abbey's construction to yet another beneficiary of the largesse of William the Conqueror, who granted the manor of Tewkesbury to his cousin, Robert Fitzhamon. In 1102 Robert began to build an abbey on the site of an

Tewkesbury Abbey

earlier Saxon foundation of which no trace survives today. The abbey still dominates the small town of Tewkesbury with its Norman crossing tower, the largest in Europe, and the abbey prospered throughout the Middle Ages, becoming one of the richest Benedictine establishments in England.

However in 1471 the abbey became an unwilling participant in one of the bloodiest episodes of the Wars of the Roses, the Battle of Tewkesbury. This battle was fought between the forces of the Houses of Lancaster and York, the contending parties for the English throne who were all descendants of Edward III. The House of York won the battle decisively, one of the House of Lancaster's casualties being the only Prince of Wales to die in battle, the 17-year-old Edward, son of the sick and helpless King Henry VI. Some Lancastrian forces sought sanctuary in the abbey afterwards but were butchered by the Yorkists, leading to the closure of the abbey and its later re-consecration. Henry VI was murdered shortly after the battle so Edward IV became

king, establishing the House of York on the throne of England.

In January 1539 Abbot John Wakeman wisely surrendered the abbey to Henry VIII and was rewarded by being made the Bishop of Gloucester, receiving an annual payment of 400 marks. The abbey was saved from destruction by the townspeople when, like those of St Albans (see 'Broken up'), they purchased it as their parish church, paying the king's commissioners a sum of £453.

UN-BROTHERLY ACTS

Edward, Prince of Wales, the son of Henry VI, is buried in Tewkesbury Abbey along with George, Duke of Clarence and brother of Edward IV. George was not a very loyal brother. He deserted his brother's Yorkist cause and sided with Henry VI, but switched sides again and was later accused by his brother King Edward IV of plotting against him. George was convicted by a Parliamentary Bill of Attainder, which without the need for anything as complicated as a trial with evidence, simply convicted him of 'unnatural, loathly treasons'.

He was subsequently 'privately executed' in the Tower of London, reputedly being upended in a barrel of Malmsey wine. Shakespeare was to lay this un-brotherly act at the door of the king's younger brother, Richard, Duke of Gloucester – later Richard III – in the poet's extremely effective assassination of that unfortunate king's character (see 'King in the car park').

TRURO CATHEDRAL

Serving Cornwall
A new diocese and a new bishop

To serve Cornwall, the new diocese of Truro was created in 1876 along with St Albans and several others to reflect the

rapid population growth in the nineteenth century. It therefore transpired that Truro Cathedral was the first to be built on a new site in Britain since Salisbury in the early thirteenth century.

The first Bishop of Truro was Edward White Benson (1829–96), who established a family of distinction within the realms of the church and elsewhere. Marrying a distant cousin he had six children: one son was the author E. F. Benson, best remembered for the *Mapp and Lucia* novels; another son, A. C. Benson, wrote the words of *Land of Hope and Glory* to Elgar's music and later became Master of Magdalene College, Cambridge; and a daughter, Margaret, became a distinguished archaeologist. Despite

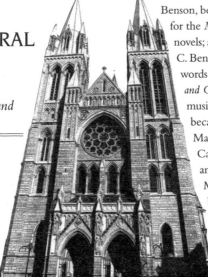

Truro Cathedral

their achievements Bishop Benson's children appear to have been affected by what we would now call bipolar disorder. None of them married, so despite having six children of their own, the bishop and his wife had no grandchildren.

The new cathedral was consecrated in November 1887, by which time Benson himself had become Archbishop of Canterbury. The building was finally completed in 1910 in the Early English Gothic style to resemble the style of Lincoln Cathedral. Benson had himself been a canon at Lincoln and the resident architect, Frank Loughborough Pearson, had been the architect of the same cathedral, also designing St Matthew's Cathedral in Auckland, New Zealand, as a smaller version of Truro.

Truro Cathedral contains a tomb much older than itself. The effigies of John Robartes, a prosperous Cornish tin merchant, and his wife Phillipa of nearby Lanhydrock House, dating from the early seventeenth century, were moved to the cathedral from the parish church that it replaced. The images are in the attitude known as lolling – elbow on the floor, head resting on hand – that was fashionable for effigies at the time. Indeed Phillipa looks thoroughly bored and possibly quite uncomfortable.

The cathedral also possesses a copy of J. H. Newman's poem 'The Dream of Gerontius', which once belonged to the decorated British army officer and administrator General Charles George Gordon (1833–85). Gordon's sister gave this to Bishop Benson after the general's death in Khartoum.

WORLDWIDE RENOWN
On Christmas Eve 1880 the new Bishop of Truro Cathedral, Edward White Benson, introduced a novel form of worship, which was designed both to arouse the interest of his rural congregation and to teach them the story of the Gospels. He designed this service working in a large wooden hut while his cathedral was being built and called it the Festival of Nine Lessons and Carols. In 1918 King's College, Cambridge adopted this service, bringing it worldwide renown through its annual broadcasts from 1928 onwards.

WELLS CATHEDRAL

Castle-like design
Hardly a traditional welcome!

For many years Wells Cathedral was embroiled in conflicts with both Bath Cathedral and Glastonbury Abbey, as these establishments disputed who should have the bishop and where he should live (see 'Decision time'). Once the argument had been resolved by papal diplomacy, Wells celebrated the final decision that the Bishop of Bath and Wells should take up residence in its small Somerset community – even the 2011 census calculated the population of Wells at less than 11,000 – by building a magnificent cathedral in the Early English Gothic style.

However the cathedral has much earlier treasures, including a Saxon font that dates from the eighth century and a choir school that dates from the time of the first Bishop of Bath and Wells – appointed in 909, he was named Athelm. His later successor Bishop Jocelin carried out much of the early work on the cathedral and the Bishop's Palace. Jocelin had been present at the

The moat around the Bishop's Palace

sealing of Magna Carta and was buried in the cathedral in 1242, the brass on his tomb being possibly the oldest in existence in England.

However the bishops of Bath and Wells, rejoicing in their new status and residence, were not content with just building a cathedral. Ralph of Shrewsbury, Bishop of Bath and Wells during the fourteenth century, built accommodation in Vicars' Close for the men who sang in the choir. He also surrounded his palace with crenellated walls and a moat, the latter filled with water diverted from streams arising from the wells that had given the city its name.

Ralph's castle-like design for his palace owed much to the strained relationship that had arisen between him and the city's citizens, who were unhappy with the exorbitant taxes levied on them to pay for the cathedral. A drawbridge over the moat was protected by a portcullis above, which was a platform from which defenders could pour boiling liquids on unwelcome visitors – hardly a traditional welcome for visitors to the bishop! The drawbridge was last used for its original purpose in

1831 when news reached Wells that the palace of the bishop of nearby Bristol had been attacked because he opposed the Great Reform Bill.

The Bishop's Palace at Wells was also used as a garrison for troops during the English Civil War (1642–51). During this the Dean of Wells, the Very Reverend Walter Raleigh – nephew of the Elizabethan explorer – was arrested and killed by his gaoler, a local cobbler and city constable, who suspected Raleigh of writing illicitly to his wife. Raleigh is buried in the cathedral. Meanwhile the Bishop's Palace itself is now classed as a Grade I listed building and is open to the public, apart from a small portion that still remains the bishop's private residence.

JUST RING FOR LUNCH

The Bishop's Palace at Wells is famous for its mute swans. In 1870 the daughter of the bishop, the Right Reverend Charles Hervey, trained them to pull on a rope to ask for food. The arrangement continues to this day and Elizabeth II, who is legally the owner of all swans in Britain, presented a pair of them to the bishop

*in 2006. The swans' lunch is served
daily to them by the caretakers.*

Unsurpassed display
Fine carvings in wood and stone

Dating from the thirteenth century, the West Front of Wells Cathedral is one of the most overwhelming spectacles on any English building by virtue of its astonishing collection of medieval statuary. It displays approximately 300 medieval statues of the highest quality, which have survived the attentions of iconoclasts throughout the centuries largely intact. Comprised of prophets and patriarchs from the Old Testament, apostles from the New Testament, figures from the history of the Christian Church in England, and some damaged figures of Christ and the Virgin Mary, this display is unsurpassed in England or anywhere else for the number

Wells Cathedral

and quality of its statues. Flakes of paint on the surface of the statues indicate that they were originally coloured, which would have made them an even more spectacular sight.

Within the cathedral are equally remarkable examples of misericords. These are carvings on the bottoms of seats that can be tipped up, allowing members of the choir and clergy to perch on them while praying or singing, thereby enabling them to 'stand' in some comfort for hours when necessary. Misericords are commonly found in the choir stalls of ancient churches but not in such profusion as at Wells, which has the finest set in Britain. Many of them in the cathedral depict animals – a cat playing with a mouse, a pair of parakeets, rabbits, monkeys, bats, mermaids and dragons – while some depict foliage and others are human figures.

Of course these misericords were designed to be unseen, since when the seats are down they are invisible and when the seats are up the people squatting on them obscure the carvings. Perhaps this helped them to survive the Protestant reformers

who were inflicting damage elsewhere within the cathedral? In any case 65 have survived the centuries, one of which is now on display in the Victoria and Albert Museum in London. Most of them were completed by the time the cathedral was ready. However the money ran out and their users were required to pay for the remaining ones to be carved – either that or stand up for eight hours a day! Their users naturally paid up.

WESTMINSTER ABBEY

Royal Peculiar
Built on an island

Westminster Abbey is unusual in being a Royal Peculiar – a church whose clergy are directly responsible to the monarch in his or her capacity as the Head of the Church of England, rather than to a bishop or archbishop. There are nine others across the land, mostly found in royal palaces such as St James's, Windsor, Holyrood and the Tower of London. However this status does not always prove advantageous. In the 1990s a dispute between the Dean of Westminster and the organist was in danger of drawing Elizabeth II into the controversy. It was therefore suggested that the Royal Peculiar status was ended – but the dispute was resolved and the status quo remained.

The exalted status of Westminster Abbey can be traced back to the reign of Edward the Confessor, who ruled England between 1042 and 1066. Crowned in Winchester, which was then the capital of Wessex, he decided to build a church at Westminster for his own burial. He chose the site of St Peter's Abbey on Thorney Island in the Thames for this, at the time a small island formed by a delta of the River Tyburn that still flows beneath the streets of London before it enters the Thames. Although no sign of the island remains, today the abbey and the Houses of Parliament accommodate its old boundaries. St Dunstan had founded St Peter's Abbey in around 960 on a site where a fisherman called Aldrich reported seeing a vision of St Peter – to this day the Fishmongers' Company annually present a salmon to the abbey.

Edward the Confessor was in the nick of time, as he died on 5 January 1066, a week after the abbey was consecrated – he was duly buried there as he had intended. Edward's abbey was the first building in England to be built in the Norman or Romanesque style, which Edward had seen in Normandy during his long period of exile there before he became king. The only part of Edward's abbey that survives today is the undercroft, now the abbey museum.

A PECULIAR PECULIAR

The little church of St Edward King and Martyr in Cambridge is the exception to the general practice of Royal Peculiars being connected to royalty. In 1441 Henry VI founded King's College, Cambridge so the church that had previously served two Cambridge Colleges, Trinity Hall and Clare, was demolished to make way for the new foundation. In compensation, Henry granted the two colleges the church of St Edward King and Martyr on Peas Hill off King's Parade, exempting it from the authority of the Bishop of Ely.

The church took advantage of this

independence during the Reformation when the ideas of reformers were openly discussed there. Indeed on Christmas Eve in 1525 a preacher named Robert Barnes gave the first openly evangelical sermon in England, accusing the Catholic Church of heresy – Henry VI, religiously a very orthodox figure, would not have been pleased. As it turned out, Barnes was later burned at the stake during the reign of Henry VI's descendant, Henry VIII.

The year of three kings
Things could only get better

1066 was the year of three kings on the English throne. Edward the Confessor was succeeded by Harold II, who was probably the first monarch crowned in Westminster Abbey. However no record of the event survives, probably because the final king to be crowned that year, William the Conqueror, had the records destroyed. However William did ensure that the abbey was portrayed in the Bayeux Tapestry, which is the famous record of his claim to the English throne and his success at taking the English throne from the unfortunate Harold at the Battle of Hastings in 1066.

William was crowned in Westminster Abbey on Christmas Day 1066 but this did not turn out to be an altogether happy occasion. When the Saxons and Normans in the abbey shouted their allegiance to the new king after his coronation, the Norman armed guards outside feared that the tumult signified rebellion and began to attack the onlooking crowd. In the words of a contemporary chronicler named Orderic Vitalis: 'The armed guard outside, hearing the tumult of the joyful crowd in the church and the harsh accents of a foreign tongue, imagined that some treachery was afoot, and rashly set fire to some of the buildings.' Not a propitious start to a reign – from this, things could only get better.

Miracle man
Shrine to the Confessor

The Westminster Abbey we see today is largely the work of Henry III, who intended it as a shrine to his Anglo-Saxon predecessor Edward the Confessor. Edward had been declared a Confessor in 1161 by Pope Alexander III, following a long campaign by Henry II, Henry III's grandfather, which cited Edward's piety and the miracles associated with him.

These miracles included the restoration of a man's sight when he was washed in water that had been previously used for Edward's royal ablutions, and the cure of a woman's skin disease. Despite these medical achievements, Edward never qualified as a saint because he was not martyred.

The Confessor's shrine, frequently moved and also despoiled by the reformers, remains a central feature of the abbey after its restoration by Mary I. The Suppression Acts of 1536 and 1539 decreed that all abbeys be dissolved, but because of the abbey's royal associations Henry VIII circumvented the act by making the abbey a cathedral, which it remained until his daughter Elizabeth I made it a Royal Peculiar.

In is interesting that the Western Towers, which are perhaps the abbey's

Edward the Confessor

most recognizable feature, are not medieval at all. Nicholas Hawksmoor added them in the eighteenth century, inspired by similar towers at Beverley Minster in Yorkshire.

Stone of Destiny
Coronations and burials at the abbey

Since 1066 coronations of the monarchs of England and the United Kingdom have invariably taken place in Westminster Abbey. And since the reign of Edward I, the Hammer of the Scots, the king or queen has been crowned sitting in King Edward's Chair, which was specially designed to accommodate the Stone of Scone, or Stone of Destiny, to emphasize the claim of English sovereigns to rule over Scotland. Edward I had stolen the stone from Scone Palace near Perth, the traditional coronation site of Scottish kings, and in 1950 some Scottish students briefly stole it in an early display of Scottish nationalism – the stone was broken during the escapade. In 1996 it was returned to Scotland but it will return once again to Westminster Abbey when future coronations take place.

In 1272 Henry III was the first king to be buried in the abbey

Coronation Chair at Westminster Abbey

since Edward the Confessor. Until the death of George II in 1760 this practice was followed for most monarchs, although since that date most have been buried in St George's Chapel at Windsor instead. It subsequently became customary to bury commoners of great distinction in the abbey, such as Isaac Newton and Charles Darwin. The latter had expected to be buried close to his home in Kent, as his family wished, but popular demand decided otherwise. So the man who had been denounced for undermining Biblical truths 23 years earlier was buried with great ceremony in the abbey, close to Newton's grave.

In 1400 Geoffrey Chaucer was buried in the abbey, not because of his poetry but because he was a royal servant – a collector of customs duties. His grave later marked the centre of what has become known as Poets' Corner, where memorials to many other artists of distinction may be found, including Henry Purcell, William Shakespeare, Charles Dickens, Thomas Hardy and Ted Hughes.

The only tomb on which no one is allowed to tread is that of

the Unknown Warrior. This was
the idea of an army chaplain, the
Reverend David Railton, and was
enthusiastically supported by the king
at the time, George V. After elaborate
precautions had been taken to ensure
that no one could identify the body
chosen from battlefields in France,
the body was conveyed to the abbey
and interred there on 11 November
1920 in the presence of the king,
two years after World War I ended.

Oliver Cromwell exhumed
Charles II takes a terrible revenge on regicide

A fter his death in 1658 Oliver
Cromwell, regicide and Lord
Protector after the execution of
Charles I, was buried with great
ceremony in Westminster Abbey.
His son Richard, nicknamed
Tumbledown Dick, briefly succeeded
him in this role but he wasn't cut
out for this position. Thus the
son of the executed monarch was
summoned back from France and
crowned Charles II in 1660.

Charles II wrought a terrible
revenge on those he held responsible
for his father's death. Any perpetrators
who still lived were hunted down
and executed, suffering the traditional
death of traitors – being hung,
drawn and quartered. In 1661
Cromwell's body was exhumed from
his grave and his head was placed
on a spike at Westminster Hall.

This head was to pass into the
hands of a succession of collectors
of gruesome curiosities. Eventually,
after being identified with 'moral
certainty', it was passed to Cromwell's
Alma Mater, Sidney Sussex College
at Cambridge, where it remains
to this day buried in a secret
place within the ante-chapel.

WINCHESTER CATHEDRAL

A bishop's displeasure
St Swithun and the weather

A t his own request Swithun,
an Anglo-Saxon Bishop of
Winchester who died in around 842
and later became a saint, was buried
outside an earlier cathedral known as

the Old Minster, which was situated just to the north of the present site. However the monks subsequently decided that his remains should be placed within the building, moving them inside on 15 July 971. On that day it rained and for 40 days that followed, a sign of Swithun's displeasure that gave rise to the verse:

St Swithun's day if thou dost rain
For forty days it will remain
St Swithun's day if thou be fair
For forty days 'twill rain nae mare

Each year on 15 July British television weather presenters can still be relied on to make reference to St Swithun and it is not surprising that he is the saint to whom we are recommended to pray in times of drought. Swithun also planted apple trees – tradition prescribes that English apples should not be picked before St Swithun's Day or they will not be ripe enough to eat.

ILLUSTRIOUS COMPANIONS
Within the Old Minster, Swithun would have joined King Alfred the
Great (849–99) and Alfred's son, Edward the Elder (874–924), as at the time of their deaths Winchester was the capital of the kingdom of Wessex. The remains of all three have long since disappeared, despite many attempts to find them. However a shrine to St Swithun remains at Winchester Cathedral, despite the destruction of an earlier version by the Tudor iconoclasts.

Walkelin's structure
Longest Gothic cathedral in Europe

In 1079 the first Norman Bishop of Winchester, Walkelin (died 1098), began the construction of the present cathedral. He used limestone brought from quarries near Fishbourne on the Isle of Wight, where many local names still reflect the excavations that took place there – Quarr Abbey, Stonelands and Stonepitts among them – and the fairways at Ryde Golf Club still bear the scars of the tracks used to transport the enormous blocks of stone.

The building was consecrated

on 8 April 1093 and Walkelin's structure has the distinction of being the longest Gothic cathedral in Europe, exceeded in length only by the classical structure of St Peter's Basilica in Rome. Its full name is the Cathedral of the Holy Trinity, Saint Peter, Saint Paul and Saint Swithun, and much of Walkelin's building survives today with much remaining Norman architecture, examples of which can be found in the crypt, the transepts and much of the nave.

However the tower collapsed as early as 1107, a misfortune attributed to the fact that William II – the son of William the Conqueror known as Rufus and a man of allegedly dissolute habits – was buried there, following his death in the nearby New Forest. The tower was rebuilt, still in the Norman style, and now has a rather squat appearance, not quite in keeping with the other dimensions of the building.

WILLIAM RUFUS
William II (1056–1100) was the third son of William the Conqueror and remains a controversial figure to this day. His nickname Rufus was

attributable to his red hair and he spent much of his reign quarrelling with the church – since it was churchmen who wrote the history of the time, this means he has received a bad press.

He was killed while hunting near Brockenhurst in the New Forest, an arrow piercing his lung, and there were suggestions that his death was not an accident. The place of his demise is marked by the Rufus Stone, which is signposted from the A31. The New Forest was seemingly a dangerous place for the Conqueror's sons – Richard, Rufus's elder brother, was also buried there after being gored by a stag in the forest.

The Clink
Bishop's private prison

The diocese of Winchester was one of the largest in England – at one time it included the Channel Islands and stretched from the south coast of England to the south bank of the Thames in Southwark. Here in Southwark the Bishop of Winchester occupied Winchester Palace, which was adjacent to the prison known as the Clink and also under the bishop's jurisdiction. These buildings are now remembered in Clink Street, which runs beneath the railway tracks leading into Cannon Street station, the Clink Prison Museum, and nearby Winchester Walk where the remains of the once magnificent palace's Rose Window may be seen.

The area was outside the jurisdiction of the City of London on the north bank of the river, thus able to accommodate theatres, brothels, cock-fighting and other entertainments of which the City fathers disapproved – hence also the need for a prison. The origins of the word 'clink' are obscure but may be owing to the clinking sound of metal caused by cell doors, keys and fetters – in any case, the word has come to be used as a generic term for prisons. A Blue Plaque commemorates the fact that the Clink Prison flourished there from 1144 and survived until 1780, when it was burned down in a riot and never rebuilt.

ILLUSTRIOUS PRISONERS
Besides the local vagrants, drunks and other undesirables, such as actors, the Clink also held some more illustrious prisoners. These included John Rogers (c. 1500–55), who was burnt at Smithfield during the reign of Mary I after being involved in publishing the Bible in English. It also briefly held some of the Pilgrim Fathers, who sailed to America in The Mayflower *in 1620.*

Wykeham's tenure
Builder, judge and first Wykehamist

Blue plaque for the Clink

Major changes to Winchester Cathedral had to wait until the fourteenth century, during the tenure of a bishop whose fame possibly surpasses that of St Swithun (see 'A bishop's displeasure'). William of Wykeham (c. 1324–1404) hailed from the village of Wickham near Fareham in Hampshire and was born of humble stock. Yet his talents attracted the support of powerful patrons, including the Constable of Winchester Castle, where he gained some experience of building that led to commissions for construction work at Windsor Castle for Edward III. This in turn led to further posts as a judge, a royal councillor and an administrator of the royal exchequer.

Ordination followed and in 1366 William became Bishop of Winchester. He used his knowledge of building to remodel the cathedral nave in the present Perpendicular style and later founded New College, Oxford and Winchester College, whose pupils are known as Wykehamists. William himself is commemorated within the cathedral in one of its many fine chapels – his effigy is decorated with angels at his head and three clerks busy at his feet, the latter representing his restless and busy life.

The fine stained glass windows that Wykeham also installed were sadly destroyed by Oliver Cromwell's forces during the English Civil War between 1642 and 1651. After Charles II was restored to the throne in 1660 the West Window was re-assembled, but such was the destruction that no attempt was made to re-assemble it in its original form. In effect the window is now an early example of the art of collage and one of the many striking features within Winchester Cathedral.

TWENTIETH-CENTURY HERO

In the early twentieth century the services of a diver named William Walker were called upon to strengthen the totally waterlogged foundations of the south and east walls of Winchester Cathedral. Thus for more than six years between 1906 and 1912 he worked in total darkness at depths of up to 6 metres (20 feet), reinforcing the foundations with 25,000 bags of concrete, 115,000 concrete blocks and almost a million bricks. His statue, of William wearing a diving suit, is to be found in the grounds of the cathedral.

Witness to history
*A royal marriage and
an author's funeral*

Winchester Cathedral has witnessed many historic events, prominent among which was the marriage of Mary I, the daughter of Henry VIII, to Philip II of Spain in 1554. This marriage took place in the cathedral because the royal couple wished to be married by Stephen Gardiner, a bishop with Catholic sympathies who had been deposed by the Protestant Edward VI then restored to his post by Mary. She did not wish to be married by the Protestant Archbishop of Canterbury, Thomas Cranmer, who later met his fate at the stake in Oxford.

The cathedral also witnessed the funeral of the writer Jane Austen, who died in Winchester at the age of 41 in 1817 and was buried in the cathedral, her funeral attended by just four people. At the time of her death she was little known as a writer and the inscription on her tomb refers simply to her benevolence and intelligence. A brass tablet now makes an understated reference to

her fame as an author, and in 1900 a memorial window was added.

WINCHESTER ON FILM
In 2005 Winchester Cathedral was used for scenes of the film **The Da Vinci Code***, based on the novel of the same name that gives a rather 'imaginative' account of Christian history – marrying Jesus to Mary Magdalene, giving them a daughter and setting off the cast in search of the Holy Grail. Moreover part of the cathedral was used as the Vatican for the film. Later the cathedral went on to host displays and debates that drew attention to the fanciful character of the novel and the film.*

WORCESTER CATHEDRAL

A fine site
*From priory to cathedral
over nine centuries*

Worcester Cathedral has a particularly fine site, its beautiful tower a prominent feature of the landscape when viewed from across the river Severn by which it stands. Like many other cathedrals such as Coventry, Worcester Cathedral

began life as a priory in about 680 but did not officially become a cathedral until Henry VIII dissolved the priory in 1540. In effect priories were small monasteries that were daughter houses of larger ones, this being the case particularly with those associated with the great Benedictine house at Cluny in Burgundy, France. One of the early priors, St Oswald, was also Bishop of Worcester from 961 to 992.

However the present building dates from 1084, having been constructed by the Anglo-Saxon Bishop

Worcester's chapter house

Chapter House Worcester Cathedral

St Wulfstan, a bishop who was almost unique in remaining in his position after the Norman Conquest – at that time William I granted most bishoprics to his Norman followers. Wulfstan left a magnificent Norman crypt and the building also has a unique chapter house, where the cathedral clergy held their meetings. Like many other Norman buildings this chapter house was built to a circular design. Yet when the walls were reinforced during the fourteenth century the external walls became octagonal, so it is now circular on the inside and an octagon outside.

John Lackland
Memorial to a bad king

The first of two royal memorials to be found at Worcester Cathedral is the tomb of King John (1199–1216), unflatteringly known during his life as Lackland owing to his unfortunate habit of losing wars against the King of France. As a result of this failure the extensive French lands bequeathed to him by his father Henry II (1154–89) and his brother Richard

I (1189–99) were lost to England.

John tried to raise money to regain his lost continental lands but his exorbitant taxes led to rebellions, the Magna Carta in 1215 (see 'Magna Carta') and eventually to the loss of his English subjects' loyalty. He died near Newark in Nottinghamshire in a final vain attempt to defeat his enemies. On his deathbed he wrote a codicil to his will that stated he would like his body to be buried in the church at Worcester.

The church was not then a cathedral but John, who spent much of his reign quarrelling with the church as with everyone else, appears to have held a particular affection for Worcester. He revered St Wulfstan and also enjoyed hunting in the forests of Feckenham in Worcestershire and Kinver, just across the border in Staffordshire. His affection for Worcester owes much to these hunting expeditions, during which he stayed at Worcester as a guest of the priory.

Like many priories, the one at Worcester was dissolved by Henry VIII and immediately became a cathedral, although this cathedral was to escape much of the destruction visited on others. Its library was dispersed and much of the contents found its way to Oxford, Cambridge and London where it may still be found – yet John's will is still held in the cathedral library. His tomb is surmounted by the first royal effigy, which is the first likeness of an English king we have.

Arthur Tudor
A death with momentous consequences

A sadder royal memorial at Worcester Cathedral is the tomb and chantry chapel dedicated to the memory of Arthur, Prince of Wales, whose death in 1502 was to have momentous consequences for the future of England and its church. Arthur was the elder son of Henry VII and in 1501, at the age of 15 years, he married Catherine of Aragon, the daughter of the King of Spain. The morning after the marriage Arthur announced that he had 'been in the midst of Spain last night', thereby implying that the marriage had been consummated –

although many have dismissed his claim as an idle boast. The young couple moved to Ludlow castle shortly afterwards and complained about the damp unhealthy air. Arthur was sickly and as a result he soon died.

Anxious to strengthen England's ties with Spain, Henry VII proposed that his second son Henry should marry his late brother's wife instead. The wedding duly took place in 1509, shortly after Henry had succeeded his father to the throne of England. There is every sign that this was at first a loving relationship, but although Catherine bore Henry six children, only one of them survived and that was a girl, Princess Mary (later Mary I). The king, anxious to produce a male heir and tiring of Catherine who was now well into her 40s and unable to produce more children, fell for the charms of the much younger Anne Boleyn.

Henry tried to persuade the Pope to annul his marriage to Catherine on the grounds that his brother had previously consummated the marriage, citing Arthur's 'In the midst of Spain' claim. However Catherine, who continued to claim until the

Arthur Tudor, the lost prince

day of her death in 1536 that she had been a virgin when she married Henry, resisted his attempts to divorce her. Despite attempts by Cardinal Thomas Wolsey to persuade him of the rightness of the king's claim, the Pope refused to annul the marriage – undoubtedly influenced by the fact that at the time the Pope was being held captive by Catherine's nephew Charles V, the Holy Roman Emperor.

Nevertheless Henry proceeded to marry Anne Boleyn with many momentous consequences: the Church of England left the Catholic fold; Thomas Wolsey lost his position as Lord Chancellor and probably escaped execution by dying just in time; and Anne Boleyn, having produced for Henry another daughter, Princess Elizabeth (later Elizabeth I), was executed within three years of her marriage to the king. If only Arthur had gone to live somewhere healthier instead!

The existence of his brother's chantry chapel may explain why Henry VIII spared Worcester the full attention of the Tudor iconoclasts, however it was less fortunate at the hands of the Puritans. After the Battle of Worcester in 1651, the final battle of the English Civil War after which Prince Charles (later Charles II) fled to his famous oak tree at Boscobel, the cathedral was vandalized by vengeful Parliamentary troops. It was not until the nineteenth century that much of the cathedral's restoration was undertaken by George Gilbert Scott (see 'An architectural dynasty').

SON OF WORCESTER TRIUMPHS

A stained glass window in Worcester Cathedral commemorates the composer Sir Edward Elgar (1857–1934), regarded by many as England's greatest composer ever, and his great work **The Dream of Gerontius.** *He was born in Worcester, the son of a piano tuner and shopkeeper who sold music and musical instruments. Much of Elgar's music was written at his home near Worcester and his first really successful composition, the* **Enigma** *Variations, received its first performance in final form at the cathedral in 1899.*

Elgar was himself a Roman Catholic at a time when they were regarded with some unease in England. Thus when he composed **The Dream of Gerontius,** *based upon a poem by Cardinal Newman about a soul's journey to heaven after death, it was met with some anxiety in Anglican circles. Nevertheless Elgar triumphed and was awarded the Order of Merit in 1911, becoming Sir Edward in 1931 and featuring on the British £20 note from 1999 to 2007. He is thus commemorated in a cathedral he would not have attended as a worshipper.*

YORK MINSTER

Bolt of lightning
The cathedral with a detachable tower

In the year 306 Constantine was proclaimed Roman emperor while campaigning in York, then known as Eboracum. It was Constantine who made Christianity the official religion of the Roman Empire, although according to the Venerable Bede (see 'Memorials') it had flourished in England for several centuries before Constantine, arriving in around 180 AD. The present cathedral, known as York Minster (see 'The King's Head'), is the fourth church on the site. The first was hurriedly built from wood in 627 to baptize Edwin, King of Northumbria in preparation for his forthcoming marriage to the Christian Princess Ethelburga of Kent.

A stone building soon followed but this was destroyed by a fire in

741 and its successor suffered the attentions of both the troublesome Vikings and an angry king, as William the Conqueror ransacked the north of England in an eventually successful attempt to subdue his discontented Saxon subjects. This was ungrateful of William since Ealdred, the Saxon Archbishop of York, had travelled to London in 1066 to crown William at his coronation in Westminster Abbey. Construction of the cathedral we now know began in William's reign

York Minster

and continued for four centuries, the consecration taking place in 1472.

The nave has a roof of wood that is painted to resemble stone, which has suffered its fair share of disasters over the centuries. In 1407 the central tower collapsed, taking with it the wooden spire that surmounted it. The tower was rebuilt but in 1967 it was found to be gradually detaching itself from the rest of the building. Medieval buildings were often constructed with very poor foundations – or often no foundations at all. This did not matter too much if they were of a uniform shape, since if the building settled with luck the whole structure would move together. However since a tower is necessarily much heavier than the surrounding structure, it is likely to settle at a faster rate, in the process becoming detached from the rest of the building.

Two million pounds was raised to stabilize the tower and strengthen the foundations, the work being completed in 1972. Twelve years later in 1984 the cathedral suffered a lightning strike, an event which caused a fire that destroyed part of the roof – this was what insurance companies once called an Act of God. Those of a superstitious disposition observed that three days earlier a new Bishop of Durham, David Jenkins, who was noted for his controversial theological opinions, had been consecrated in the cathedral – others thought it was chance. The roof was replaced and partly decorated with designs by the winners of *Blue Peter,* a BBC television programme.

ARSON ATTACK

Lightning was not the only cause of fire that was to damage York Minster. In 1829 Jonathan Martin, a native of Hexham in Northumberland, launched an arson attack on the cathedral. After a troubled upbringing – he saw his sister murdered by a neighbour and was press-ganged into the Royal Navy, serving under Admiral Nelson at the battle of Copenhagen – Martin became a Wesleyan preacher with a marked hostility towards the Church of England.

After threatening to shoot the Bishop of Oxford he was sent to a lunatic asylum, subsequently escaping and offering his services to the Wesleyans who wisely declined his offer. During evensong in York Minster in February 1829 he was disturbed by the sound of the organ and later set fire to the building. After being tried at York at a time when arson was punishable by a death sentence the judge declared him insane – Martin was sent to the Bethlem asylum where he died nine years later.

Walls of glass
Saved by a Tudor Rose

York Minster is one of the few English churches whose painted glass, consisting of some two million separate pieces in 128 windows, survived the attention of both the Tudors and the Cromwellian Puritans almost intact. The Five Sisters Window in the north transept would be regarded as extraordinary in almost any other building. Yet the Great East Window surpasses it, as the largest expanse of medieval painted glass in the world. Meanwhile the West Window is known as the Heart of Yorkshire.

This astonishing glass may owe its survival to a Rose Window in the south transept. Dating from around 1500, this window commemorates the marriage of Henry VII, a descendant of the House of Lancaster, to Elizabeth of York thus ending the Wars of the Roses that had disfigured much of the previous century in England. The window comprises panels of the Tudor Rose, unknown to botany but common in heraldry

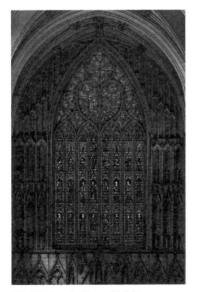

West Window, the Heart of Yorkshire

of the period, which consists of a red rose for Lancaster with a white rose for York superimposed at its centre. Henry VIII, the son of Henry VII and Elizabeth, possibly spared the cathedral the destruction meted out to others because it contained this beautiful memorial to his own parents.

The glass had another narrow escape in 1644 when York fell into the hands of Parliamentary forces after the Battle of Marston Moor outside the city, the decisive blow being made by a cavalry charge led by Oliver Cromwell. The city was surrendered to the Parliamentary commander, Thomas Fairfax, on condition that the cathedral remained undamaged. Fairfax proved more trustworthy than Henry VIII (see 'Rebellious Yorkshiremen') – the glass was spared.

Rebellious Yorkshiremen
York Minster churchmen join the fray

Despite Henry VIII's forbearance over their windows at York Minster (see 'Walls of glass'), the folk of Yorkshire proved rather ungrateful to their king. In 1536 the Pilgrimage of Grace rose in Yorkshire, preceded by a similar movement in Lincolnshire, as a protest against the break with Rome – in particular the activities of Thomas Cromwell in closing monasteries and desecrating churches. Cromwell had particularly offended the people of Yorkshire by damaging the shrine of the former Archbishop of York, St William Fitzherbert, which had become popular with pilgrims and was therefore a source of wealth to the cathedral and city of York.

A man named Robert Aske led the rebellion and occupied York with 9,000 followers, inviting the expelled monks and nuns to return. He eventually assembled four times that number near Doncaster, where Henry VIII sent the Duke of Norfolk to negotiate with them. The Duke promised an amnesty on behalf of Henry, but once the rebels had dispersed their leaders were arrested and executed for treason. This was the most serious uprising ever to occur against the Tudor dynasty, although it was not the first serious rebellion to occur in Yorkshire.

After the deposition of King Richard II in 1399 and his death soon afterwards in Pontefract Castle, one of the cathedral's canons who resembled the late king attempted to impersonate him and lead a rebellion. No one was fooled, although a further rebellion by the Archbishop of York, Richard Scrope, against Henry IV in 1405 gained some support. However not enough – Scrope was tried and condemned in his own palace then subsequently executed.

SUMMONED BY BELLS

York Minster is particularly well served by its bells. The north-west tower holds Great Peter, which weighs almost 11 tons, as well as six bells for its clock that chime every 15 minutes, Great Peter striking the hours. The south-west tower accommodates 14 bells for change ringing and the cathedral also has a carillon – a set of 35 bells that can be played from a keyboard and used for anything from hymn tunes to popular music.

GLOSSARY TO ECCLESIASTICAL ARCHITECTURE

Every attempt has been made in this book to avoid the use of language that requires specialist knowledge of architecture, however the following terms are used in the sense briefly described.

Aisles: Passages found on either side of the nave.

Canon: A clergyman who works in and manages the affairs of a cathedral.

Chancel: The area in front of the altar, occupied by the choir.

Chantry chapel: A chapel within a cathedral endowed to say masses for the soul of the donor.

Chapter house: A building used by the governing body of the cathedral for meetings.

Classical architecture: A style based upon the Greek and Roman models, using materials and construction techniques of later centuries.

Classical Baroque architecture: A European style of the seventeenth and eighteenth century that is more elaborate and expressive than the simpler Classical

architecture – Christopher Wren's St Paul's Cathedral in London is a good example.

Clerestory: The upper section of the wall of the nave, the choir and transepts, usually with windows.

Corbel: A small carving, often found at the top of a pillar and featuring the head of a human or small animal.

Crypt: A room or vault beneath a church, normally used to hold a collection of sarcophagi.

Dean: The clergyman in charge of the cathedral, sometimes called a **provost**.

Friar: Similar to a monk but is based in a friary and travels about in the surrounding community to preach the gospel. The largest orders of friars are the Franciscans, the Dominicans and the Augustinians, who follow the teachings of St Francis of Assisi, St Dominic and St Augustine of Hippo respectively, and all originate in the thirteenth century.

Gothic architecture: A style that dates from the twelfth century and is characterized by pointed arches and elaborate stone carving. It is divided into: **Early English**, with narrow arches and windows known as lancets, as at Salisbury Cathedral; **Decorated**, with broader arches and more elaborate

carving, as at York Minster; and
Perpendicular, with narrow soaring columns and often fan vaulting, as at Gloucester Cathedral.

Lady Chapel: A chapel dedicated to the Virgin Mary, usually found at the east end of a cathedral.

Lectern: A tall stand used in a cathedral as a reading desk on which the Bible and other books are laid while they are being read to the congregation.

Misericord: A carved figure on the bottom of a seat that can be tipped up, allowing a member of the choir or clergy to perch on it while praying or singing. This enabled them to appear to be standing for hours if necessary, while retaining some comfort.

Modern architecture: This comes in many forms, taking advantage of developments in materials and engineering techniques. The outstanding example is Coventry Cathedral, which was completed in 1962 to a design by Sir Basil Spence.

Monk and nun: A male or female member of a religious community – a man living in a monastery and a woman in a convent – who follows a religious vocation. Most base their way of life on the rules of St Benedict of Nursia (c. 480

– c. 543), living under vows based on the virtues of poverty, chastity and obedience.

Nave: The main central body of a cathedral, usually aligned from east to west.

Rose window: A circular window, usually very large and suggestive of a rose, which contains elaborate stained glass designs.

Sarcophagus: A stone coffin that usually remains unburied in a cathedral or another place of worship, which is often used as a receptacle for the body of an eminent person.

Transepts: The areas within a cathedral that project at right angles to the nave, often beneath the tower, to form a cross – a tower positioned thus is called a **crossing tower**.

Triforium: A narrow arched gallery that runs above and along the nave, often within the clerestory.

Undercroft: A vaulted basement in a cathedral usually used for storage – Westminster Abbey has a particularly fine one.

Vault: The ceiling beneath the roof of a church, made of wood, or a cathedral, often made of finely carved stone.

INDEX

Amazing and Extraordinary
Facts: London
Stephen Halliday
ISBN: 978-1-910821-02-2

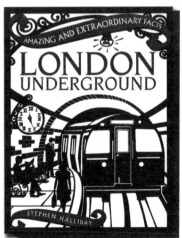

Amazing and Extraordinary
Facts: London Underground
Stephen Halliday
ISBN: 978-1-910821-03-9

Amazing and Extraordinary
Facts: The English
Countryside
Ruth Binney
ISBN: 978-1-910821-01-5

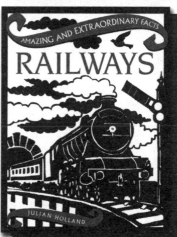

Amazing and Extraordinary
Facts: Railways
Julian Holland
ISBN: 978-1-910821-00-8

For more great books visit our website at **www.rydonpublishing.co.uk**

THE AUTHOR

Stephen Halliday is a historian specializing in British and industrial history. He is an authority on the history of London with a special interest in its great engineering works, and he is the author of several books about London and the Underground including *Amazing and Extraordinary Facts: London*. He also contributes articles and reviews to magazines such as *Literary Review, Times Higher Education, BBC History* and *History Today*.

PICTURE CREDITS

Images on following pages adapted from work by:
pg10 Unknown artist; pg12 Unknown artist; pg15 Archiseek.com; pg18 British Library; pg19 Photograph by Michael Maggs, Original artist unknown; pg25 amazon.com/images; pg27 Engraved by J. LeKeux after a picture by G. Cattermole; pg30 British Library; pg31 Stephen Hamilton; pg33 Tony Hisgett; pg35 Elliott Brown; pg36 Wolfgang Sauber; pg40 mattbuck; pg43 John Salmon; pg44 Etching by R.W. Smart; pg46 David Iliff; pg49 Mark Broadhurst; pg52 Ad Meskens; pg53 John Slezer; pg55 Nilfanion; pg56 Stukeley; pg58 William Avery; pg60 EdwardII-Cassell; pg63 Hereford Mappa Mundi 1300 Briangotts; pg64 Poliphilo; pg66 Isananni; pg67 Wenceslaus Hollar; pg68 Richard Croft; pg71 Rainer Ebert; pg73 Chowells; pg76 Humphrey Bolton; pg77 Unknown artist; pg78 Bain; pg80 Sampson Strong; pg82 Lyricmac; pg85 Unknown artist; pg91 Unknown artist; pg93 George P. Landow; pg95 Lucas Hornebolte; pg97 Hans Holbein the Younger; pg99 Melancholia; pg101 John Constable; pg102 British Library; pg105 Claes Van Visscher; pg106 Wenceslaus Hollar; pg108 Anthony van Dyck; pg109 W. Lloyd MacKenzie; pg111 Edward Webb; pg113 David Fox; pg115 seier+seier; pg119 Myrabella; pg120 Anonymous engraver; pg124 Spudgun67; pg127 Rock & Co; pg130 Unknown artist; pg132 Mark A. Wilson; pg134 David Iliff